America's BEST RECIPES

Comfort Food

175 Made-with-Love Family Favorite Recipes

Double Apple Pie with
Cornmeal Crust,
page 248

Comfort Food

175 Made-with-Love Family Favorite Recipes

Oxmoor House®

ISBN-13: 978-0-8487-3692-7
ISBN-10: 0-8487-3692-3
Library of Congress Control Number: 2012930913

Printed in the United States of America
First Printing 2012

Oxmoor House

VP, Publishing Director: Jim Childs
Creative Director: Felicity Keane
Senior Brand Manager: Daniel Fagan
Senior Editor: Rebecca Brennan
Managing Editor: Rebecca Benton

America's Best Recipes Comfort Food

Project Editor: Sarah H. Doss
Assistant Designer: Allison S. Potter
Director, Test Kitchen: Elizabeth Tyler Austin
Assistant Directors, Test Kitchen:
   Julie Christopher, Julie Gunter
Test Kitchen Professionals: Wendy Ball, R.D.;
   Allison E. Cox; Victoria E. Cox; Margaret
   Monroe Dickey; Alyson Moreland Haynes;
   Stefanie Maloney; Callie Nash; Catherine
   Crowell Steele; Leah Van Deren
Photography Director: Jim Bathie
Senior Photo Stylist: Kay E. Clarke
Photo Stylist: Katherine Eckert Coyne
Assistant Photo Stylist: Mary Louise Menendez
Production Manager: Theresa Beste-Farley
Assistant Production Manager: Diane Rose

Contributors

Editor: Jessica Cox
Copy Editor: Donna Baldone
Proofreaders: Julie Bosché, Mary Ann Laurens
Indexer: Nanette Cardon
Interns: Erin Bishop, Maribeth Browning,
   Mackenzie Cogle, Laura Hoxworth, Alicia
   Lavender, Anna Pollock, Ashley White
Test Kitchen Professionals: Martha Condra, Erica
   Hopper, Kathleen Royal Phillips
Photographer: Mary Britton Senseney
Photo Stylist: Mindi Shapiro Levine

Time Home Entertainment Inc.

Publisher: Richard Fraiman
VP, Strategy & Business Development:
   Steven Sandonato
Executive Director, Marketing Services:
   Carol Pittard
Executive Director, Retail & Special Sales:
   Tom Mifsud
Director, Bookazine Development & Marketing:
   Laura Adam
Publishing Director: Joy Butts
Finance Director: Glenn Buonocore
Associate General Counsel: Helen Wan

To order additional publications, call
1-800-765-6400 or 1-800-491-0551.

For more books to enrich your life, visit
oxmoorhouse.com
To search, savor, and share thousands of recipes, visit **myrecipes.com**

Cover: Buttermilk Picnic Chicken (page 32)
Back Cover: 30-Minute Chili (page 58),
Triple-Decker Strawberry Cake (page 236),
Pimiento Cheese Biscuits (page 127)

welcome

Macaroni and cheese, meatloaf, mashed potatoes—some foods do more than fill the stomach. They have the ability to transport us to a specific time and place, to fill us with nostalgia, and to convey the love of the hands that prepared them. Take a trip down Memory Lane with this soul-satisfying collection of comfort food favorites.

Here you'll find **more than 100 sure-to-please recipes** that have been fully tested by our staff of professional cooks, so you can rest assured they'll turn out perfectly every time. You'll be prepared with just the right dish to warm your family's hearts as you gather around the table to recall special memories and make new ones.

With menus for **Weeknight Family Meals** and **Quick & Easy Homestyle** recipes, dinner can be on the table in no time. From our best crowd-pleasing dishes for **Casual Entertaining** to **Breads, Breakfast & Brunch,** plus a selection of **Main Dishes, Side Dishes,** and **Sweet Endings,** you're sure to find all the foods you crave, plus a few new favorites. You'll also discover useful notes from our test kitchen and serving suggestions to make menu planning even simpler.

Our hope is that the recipes in this book will give you just what you need to **prepare wholesome, comforting meals no matter the occasion**. So sit back and enjoy; let your heart and home be warmed by these comforting, cherished dishes.

From our kitchen to yours,

Jessica Cox
Editor

Cinnamon-Pecan Rolls,
page 139

Contents

Grilled Baby Back Ribs,
page 177

Corn Pudding,
page 203

Pound Cake Banana
Pudding, page 262

Chapter 1

WEEKNIGHT FAMILY MEALS

Gonzales Meatloaf

makes 6 to 8 servings ☆ prep: 15 min. ☆ cook: 1 hr. ☆ stand: 10 min.

pictured on page 8

Cilantro, brown sugar, and a heavy shake of hot sauce deliver big flavor to this meatloaf. Leftovers make a great sandwich.

2 lb. **ground sirloin**
3 large **eggs**, lightly beaten
1 cup fine, dry **breadcrumbs**
4 **garlic cloves,** minced
1 medium-size **red onion,** chopped
2 **plum tomatoes,** seeded and chopped
1½ cups (6 oz.) shredded **Monterey Jack cheese**

¼ to ½ cup firmly packed **brown sugar**
½ cup chopped **fresh cilantro**
¼ cup **Worcestershire sauce**
2 Tbsp. **hot sauce**
2 tsp. **salt**
1 tsp. **pepper**

1. Preheat oven to 350°. Combine all ingredients. Shape into a free-form 9- x 5-inch loaf, and place on a lightly greased rack in a broiler pan.

2. Bake at 350° for 45 minutes; increase oven temperature to 425°, and bake 15 to 25 more minutes or until done. Let meatloaf stand 10 minutes before serving.

serve with

Home-Cooked Pole Beans

makes 8 servings ☆ prep: 26 min. ☆ cook: 19 min. ☆ pictured on page 8

2 lb. **fresh pole beans**
3 **bacon** slices
1 tsp. **salt**

½ tsp. **pepper**
¼ tsp. **sugar**

1. Wash beans; trim stem ends. Cut beans into 1½-inch pieces, and set aside.

2. Cook bacon in a large saucepan until crisp; remove bacon, reserving drippings in pan. Crumble bacon, and set aside.

3. Add 1 cup water and remaining 3 ingredients to saucepan; bring to a boil over high heat. Add beans; cover, reduce heat to medium, and cook 15 minutes or to desired doneness. Sprinkle with crumbled bacon. Serve with a slotted spoon.

serve with

Buttermilk-Garlic Mashed Potatoes

makes 4 servings ☆ prep: 10 min. ☆ cook: 6 min. ☆ pictured on page 8

2 Tbsp. **butter**
3 **garlic cloves,** chopped
2 cups **buttermilk**
⅔ cup **milk**
½ tsp. **salt**
½ tsp. **pepper**
1 (22-oz.) package **frozen mashed potatoes**

1. Melt butter in a Dutch oven over medium heat; add garlic, and sauté 1 minute.

2. Add buttermilk and next 3 ingredients. Cook, stirring constantly, 5 minutes or until thoroughly heated. Stir in potatoes until smooth.

Note: We tested with Ore-Ida Mashed Potatoes. There's no need to thaw them. This recipe doubles easily to serve 8.

Smothered Swiss Steak

makes 6 servings ☆ prep: 15 min. ☆ cook: 1 hr., 19 min.

½ tsp. **salt**
6 (4-oz.) **cube steaks**
½ cup **all-purpose flour**
1 tsp. **seasoned pepper**
4½ Tbsp. **vegetable oil**
1 medium **onion,** diced
1 medium-size **green bell pepper,** diced
1 (14.5-oz.) can **petite diced tomatoes**
1 (12-oz.) **can cola soft drink**
1 Tbsp. **beef bouillon granules**
2 Tbsp. **tomato paste**

A cola soft drink is the secret ingredient for these slow-cooked steaks with a juicy tomato-based sauce. Start table talk by asking everyone to guess the surprise flavoring. For a complete meal, serve with rice to soak up all of the delicious sauce and an iceberg wedge salad.

1. Sprinkle salt evenly on both sides of cube steaks. Combine flour and pepper in a shallow dish. Dredge cube steaks in flour mixture.

2. Brown 2 steaks in 1½ Tbsp. hot oil in a large nonstick skillet over medium-high heat 3 minutes on each side; drain on paper towels. Repeat procedure with remaining steaks and oil. Drain drippings from skillet, reserving 1 Tbsp. in skillet.

3. Sauté onion and bell pepper in hot drippings 7 minutes or until tender. Add diced tomatoes and remaining 3 ingredients. Bring to a boil, and cook, stirring often, 5 minutes or until slightly thickened. Return steaks to skillet; cover and cook over low heat 55 to 60 minutes or until tender.

make ahead

To prepare this recipe in a slow cooker, place seared cube steaks in a 5-qt. slow cooker. After cola mixture has cooked 5 minutes, spoon it over seared cube steaks. Cover and cook on LOW 5 hours.

Grilled Steak and Vegetable Kabobs

makes 4 servings ☆ prep: 20 min. ☆ cook: 12 min. ☆ chill: 20 min.

Fire up the grill and have steak on the table in less than an hour with these simple yet flavorful kabobs. Your kids might even eat their vegetables when they come on a stick.

1½ Tbsp. **honey**	1 large **sweet onion,** cut into ½-inch wedges
1½ Tbsp. **soy sauce**	1 (8-oz.) package **fresh mushrooms**
1 Tbsp. **olive oil**	
¼ tsp. **salt**	1 medium-size **green bell pepper,** cut into 1-inch cubes
1 lb. **flat-iron steaks,** cut into 1-inch cubes	
8 (7- to 8-inch) **wooden skewers**	**Salt** and **pepper** to taste

1. Preheat grill to 350° to 400° (medium-high) heat. Whisk together first 4 ingredients in a large shallow dish or combine in a zip-top plastic freezer bag; add beef, turning to coat. Cover, or seal bag, and chill 20 minutes, turning once.

2. Meanwhile, soak the wooden skewers in water 10 minutes.

3. Remove beef from marinade, discarding marinade. Thread beef onto 4 skewers, onion onto 2 skewers, and mushrooms and peppers onto remaining 2 skewers. Sprinkle kabobs with desired amount of salt and pepper.

4. Grill beef and vegetables at the same time, covered with grill lid. Grill beef 6 minutes on each side or to desired degree of doneness. Grill vegetables 10 minutes or until tender, turning occasionally.

simple side

Zesty Zucchini: Cut 2 large zucchini into 2-inch-long sticks. Place on an aluminum foil–lined baking sheet, and toss with 1 Tbsp. olive oil and 1 tsp. salt. Bake at 425° for 25 minutes or until browned, turning once.

Cheesy Chili Hash Brown Bake

makes 8 servings ☆ prep: 12 min. ☆ cook: 52 min.

Three comfort foods converge in this five-ingredient homestyle favorite.

1½ lb. **lean ground beef** or **turkey**
1 (15.5-oz.) can **original sloppy Joe sauce**
1 (15-oz.) can **chili with beans**
½ (30-oz.) package **frozen country-style shredded hash browns** (about 4 cups)
2 cups (8 oz.) shredded **Cheddar cheese**

1. Preheat oven to 425°. Brown ground beef in a large skillet over medium-high heat, stirring often, 7 to 10 minutes or until meat crumbles and is no longer pink. Stir in sloppy Joe sauce and chili.

2. Spoon chili mixture into 8 lightly greased 10-oz. ramekins. Top with frozen hash browns.

3. Bake, covered, at 425° for 30 minutes; uncover and bake 10 more minutes or until browned and crisp. Sprinkle with cheese and bake 5 more minutes or until cheese is melted.

Note: We tested with Manwich Original Sloppy Joe Sauce and Hormel Chili with Beans. Chili mixture can be baked in a lightly greased 13- x 9-inch baking dish.

simple side

Lemony Broccoli: Cook 1 (10-oz.) package frozen broccoli spears in butter sauce according to package directions. Sprinkle with ½ tsp. lemon pepper.

Slow-Cooker BBQ Pork

makes 6 servings ☆ prep: 5 min. ☆ cook: 6 hr.

1   (3- to 4-lb.) **shoulder pork roast**
1   (18-oz.) bottle **barbecue sauce**
1   (12-oz.) can **cola soft drink**

This super-simple recipe delivers big flavor. Let it cook all day in your slow cooker and have a homemade meal ready when you walk in the door.

1. Place pork roast in a 6-qt. slow cooker; pour barbecue sauce and cola over roast.

2. Cover with lid, and cook on HIGH 6 to 7 hours or until meat is tender and shreds easily. Serve on buns with slaw or over hot toasted cornbread.

Note: We tested with Sticky Fingers Memphis Original Barbecue Sauce. If you don't have a slow cooker, place roast in a lightly greased Dutch oven; stir together barbecue sauce and cola, and pour over roast. Before placing lid on top of Dutch oven, cover roast with a double layer of aluminum foil. Bake, tightly covered, at 325° for 3½ hours or until tender.

serve with

Memphis-Style Coleslaw

makes 12 servings ☆ prep: 7 min. ☆ chill: 2 hr.

2   cups **mayonnaise**
¼   cup **sugar**
¼   cup **Dijon mustard**
¼   cup **cider vinegar**
1½   to 2 Tbsp. **celery seeds**
1   tsp. **salt**
⅛   tsp. **pepper**
1   medium **cabbage**, shredded, or 3 (10-oz.) bags finely shredded **cabbage**
2   large **carrots**, grated
1   **green bell pepper,** diced
2   Tbsp. grated **onion**

1. Stir together first 7 ingredients in a large bowl; add cabbage and remaining ingredients, tossing gently. Cover and chill 2 to 3 hours; serve with a slotted spoon.

Bourbon-Brown Sugar Pork Tenderloin

makes 6 to 8 servings ☆ prep: 14 min. ☆ cook: 17 min. ☆ other: 8 hr., 10 min.

Here's a fresh, weeknight-easy spin on Sunday pork roast with gravy. A quick reduction transforms the flavorful marinade into an indulgent sauce. Add a burst of color to this meal by serving with green beans, if desired.

2	(1-lb.) **pork tenderloins***
¼	cup firmly packed **dark brown sugar**
¼	cup minced **green onions**
¼	cup **bourbon**
¼	cup **soy sauce**
¼	cup **Dijon mustard**
½	tsp. freshly ground **pepper**
½	tsp. **cornstarch**

1. Remove silver skin from tenderloins, leaving a thin layer of fat. Combine brown sugar and next 5 ingredients in a large zip-top plastic freezer bag; add pork. Seal bag, and chill 8 to 18 hours, turning bag occasionally. Remove pork from marinade, reserving marinade.

2. Preheat grill to 350° to 400° (medium-high) heat. Grill pork, covered with grill lid, 8 minutes on each side or until a meat thermometer inserted into thickest portion registers 155°. Remove from grill, and let stand 10 minutes.

3. Meanwhile, combine reserved marinade and cornstarch in a saucepan. Bring to a boil over medium heat; cook, stirring constantly, 1 minute. Cut pork diagonally into thin slices, and arrange on a serving platter; drizzle with warm sauce.

* 1½ lb. flank steak may be substituted. Reduce grill time to 6 to 8 minutes on each side or to desired degree of doneness.

serve with

Garlic-Chive Mashed Potatoes

makes 6 servings ☆ prep: 10 min. ☆ cook: 10 min.

24 oz. pkg. **frozen steam-and-mash potatoes**
1 Tbsp. **butter**
4 **garlic cloves,** minced
4 oz. **fat-free cream cheese**

⅔ cup **fat-free milk**
⅓ cup chopped **fresh chives**
Salt and freshly ground **pepper** to taste

A swirl of fat-free cream cheese turns hot mashed potatoes into a deceptively rich side dish.

1. Microwave frozen steam-and-mash potatoes according to package directions. Meanwhile, melt 1 Tbsp. butter in a small skillet over medium heat; add minced garlic cloves, and sauté 1 minute.

2. Transfer cooked potatoes to a large bowl. Add garlic mixture, fat-free cream cheese, fat-free milk, chopped fresh chives, and salt and freshly ground pepper to taste; mash potato mixture to desired consistency.

Note: We tested with Ore-Ida Steam n' Mash Cut Russet Potatoes.

serve with

Skillet Cornbread

makes 8 servings ☆ prep: 10 min. ☆ cook: 30 min.

2 tsp. **canola oil**
1¾ cups **self-rising white cornmeal mix**
2 cups **nonfat buttermilk**

¼ cup **all-purpose flour**
1 large **egg,** lightly beaten
2 Tbsp. melted **butter**
1 Tbsp. **sugar**

1. Preheat oven to 425°.

2. Coat bottom and sides of a 10-inch cast-iron skillet with 2 tsp. canola oil; heat in oven 5 minutes.

3. Meanwhile, whisk together self-rising white cornmeal mix, nonfat buttermilk, all-purpose flour, egg, melted butter, and sugar. Pour batter into hot skillet. Bake 25 to 30 minutes until golden.

Oven-Fried Pork Chops with Roasted Green Beans and Pecans

makes 4 servings ☆ prep: 7 min. ☆ cook: 33 min.

This quick and satisfying meal is sure to bring comfort to the weariest of midweek souls. Serve with warm dinner rolls.

2   (12-oz.) packages **fresh cut green beans**
1   Tbsp. **olive oil**
1   tsp. **salt**, divided
4   (4- to 6-oz.) **bone-in center-cut pork chops**
¼   tsp. **pepper**
½   cup **Japanese breadcrumbs (panko)**

¼   cup freshly grated **Parmesan cheese**
1   Tbsp. **lemon zest**
1   tsp. chopped **fresh thyme**
¼   cup **vegetable oil**
¼   cup chopped **pecans**
½   Tbsp. **butter**

1. Preheat oven to 450°. Drain and rinse beans. Combine beans, 1 Tbsp. olive oil, and ¾ tsp. salt in a large bowl, tossing to coat. Spread beans in a single layer in a jelly-roll pan. Bake 18 to 20 minutes or until beans are tender and slightly browned.

2. Meanwhile, sprinkle pork chops with pepper and remaining ¼ tsp. salt. Stir together breadcrumbs and next 3 ingredients in a large shallow dish. Dredge pork chops in breadcrumb mixture.

3. Cook chops in ¼ cup hot vegetable oil in a large skillet over medium heat 5 to 6 minutes on each side or until done.

4. Stir pecans and butter into beans; bake 5 to 6 more minutes or until pecans are golden. Serve pork chops with green beans.

Onion-Topped Sausage 'n' Mashed Potato Casserole

makes 6 servings ☆ prep: 15 min. ☆ cook: 51 min. ☆ stand: 5 min.

1 (19.5-oz.) package **sweet ground turkey sausage, casings removed***

2 (14.5-oz.) cans **diced tomatoes in sauce**

¼ cup loosely packed **fresh basil leaves**, chopped**

1 **shallot**, chopped

1 tsp. **salt-free garlic-and-herb seasoning**

1 (24-oz.) package **refrigerated garlic-flavored mashed potatoes**

1 (8-oz.) package shredded **Italian five-cheese blend**

¼ tsp. **dried Italian seasoning**

1 cup **French fried onions**

Nothing says comfort like a cheesy, crispy-topped casserole. Serve this soon-to-be family favorite with sautéed green beans.

1. Preheat oven to 350°. Brown sausage in a large skillet over medium-high heat, stirring often, 6 to 8 minutes or until meat crumbles and is no longer pink; drain.

2. Stir in tomatoes and next 3 ingredients, and cook, stirring occasionally, 5 minutes. Transfer sausage mixture to a lightly greased 11- x 7-inch baking dish.

3. Stir together mashed potatoes, cheese, and Italian seasoning in a large bowl. (Mixture will be dry.) Spread potato mixture over sausage mixture in baking dish.

4. Bake at 350° for 35 to 40 minutes or until bubbly. Top with fried onions, and bake 5 more minutes. Let stand 5 minutes before serving.

*1 (1¼-lb.) package ground chicken sausage may be substituted.

**1 tsp. dried basil may be substituted.

Ham-and-Greens Pot Pie with Cornbread Crust

makes 8 to 10 servings ☆ prep: 15 min. ☆ cook: 44 min. ☆ stand: 10 min.

Traditionally eaten on New Year's Day for good luck and riches in the coming year, collard greens and black-eyed peas are an all-star combination in this casserole topped with a crumbly cornbread crust.

4 cups chopped **cooked ham**
2 Tbsp. **vegetable oil**
3 Tbsp. **all-purpose flour**
3 cups **chicken broth**
1 (16-oz.) package **frozen diced onion, red and green bell pepper, and celery,** thawed
1 (16-oz.) package **frozen chopped collard greens**
1 (16-oz.) can **black-eyed peas,** drained and rinsed
½ tsp. **dried crushed red pepper**
Cornbread Crust Batter

1. Preheat oven to 425°.

2. Sauté ham in hot oil in a Dutch oven over medium-high heat 5 minutes or until lightly browned. Add flour, and cook, stirring constantly, 1 minute. Gradually add chicken broth, and cook, stirring constantly, 3 minutes or until broth begins to thicken.

3. Bring mixture to a boil, and add frozen diced onion, pepper, and celery blend and collard greens; return to a boil, and cook, stirring often, 15 minutes. Stir in black-eyed peas and crushed red pepper; spoon hot mixture into a lightly greased 13- x 9-inch baking dish.

4. Pour Cornbread Crust Batter over hot filling mixture. Bake at 425° for 20 to 25 minutes or until cornbread is golden brown and set. Let stand 10 minutes before serving.

Note: We tested with Pictsweet Seasoning Blend for frozen diced vegetables.

make ahead

To get a head start on this recipe, make it a day in advance through Step 3; cover and refrigerate. The following day, simply reheat the filling in the microwave; uncover and continue with Step 4.

Cornbread Crust Batter

makes enough batter for 1 (13- x 9-inch) pan ☆ crust prep: 10 min.

1½ cups **white cornmeal mix**
½   cup **all-purpose flour**
1   tsp. **sugar**

2   large **eggs,** lightly beaten
1½ cups **buttermilk**

1. Combine first 3 ingredients; make a well in the center of mixture. Add eggs and buttermilk to cornmeal mixture, stirring just until moistened.

Grilled Chicken with Corn and Slaw

makes 4 servings ☆ prep: 9 min. ☆ cook: 14 min.

1   cup **mayonnaise**
¼   cup chopped **fresh cilantro**
6   Tbsp. **white wine vinegar,** divided
¾   tsp. **salt,** divided
⅛   tsp. **pepper**
4   **skinless, boneless chicken breasts** (about 1 lb.)
4   ears **fresh corn,** husks removed

¼   cup melted **butter**
1   (10-oz.) package **shredded coleslaw mix**
3   Tbsp. **olive oil**
½   tsp. **sugar**
¼   tsp. **pepper**
Salt and **pepper** to taste

Fire up the grill and head outside for a no-fuss cookout with this light summertime trio.

1. Combine mayonnaise, cilantro, 3 Tbsp. vinegar, ¼ tsp. salt, and ⅛ tsp. pepper in a small bowl. Reserve ¾ cup mayonnaise mixture. Brush chicken with remaining ¼ cup mayonnaise mixture.

2. Preheat grill to 350° to 400° (medium-high) heat. Grill chicken and corn at the same time, covered with grill lid. Grill chicken 7 to 10 minutes on each side or until done; grill corn 14 to 20 minutes or until done, turning every 4 to 5 minutes and basting with melted butter.

3. Toss coleslaw mix with oil, sugar, ¼ tsp. pepper, and remaining 3 Tbsp. vinegar and ½ tsp. salt. Season chicken and corn with salt and pepper to taste. Serve with coleslaw and reserved mayonnaise mixture.

Chicken Tetrazzini

makes 12 servings ☆ prep: 20 min. ☆ cook: 35 min.

Tetrazzini is a house-favorite cheese-and-chicken entrée. This version serves plenty.

1 (16-oz.) package **vermicelli**
½ cup **chicken broth**
4 cups chopped **cooked chicken**
1 (10¾-oz.) can **cream of mushroom soup**
1 (10¾-oz.) can **cream of chicken soup**
1 (10¾-oz.) can **cream of celery soup**
1 (8-oz.) container **sour cream**
1 (6-oz.) jar sliced **mushrooms**, drained
½ cup (2 oz.) shredded **Parmesan cheese**
1 tsp. **pepper**
½ tsp. **salt**
2 cups (8 oz.) shredded **Cheddar cheese**

1. Cook vermicelli according to package directions; drain. Return to pot, and toss with chicken broth.

2. Preheat oven to 350°. Stir together chopped cooked chicken and next 8 ingredients in a large bowl; add vermicelli, and toss well. Spoon chicken mixture into 2 lightly greased 11- x 7-inch baking dishes. Sprinkle with Cheddar cheese.

3. Bake, covered, at 350° for 30 minutes; uncover and bake 5 more minutes or until cheese is bubbly.

make ahead

This speedy Italian classic can be made ahead for an easy and delicious weeknight dinner. Freeze unbaked casserole up to 1 month, if desired. Thaw casserole overnight in refrigerator. Let stand 30 minutes at room temperature, and bake as directed.

Buttermilk Picnic Chicken

makes 6 to 8 servings ☆ prep: 25 min. ☆ cook: 1 hr. ☆ other: 8 hr.

Think "picnic" when you prepare this seasoned chicken marinated in buttermilk. If the weather doesn't cooperate, spread a blanket on the den floor and have an indoor picnic.

¾	cup **buttermilk**
2	tsp. **chicken bouillon granules**
1	tsp. **poultry seasoning**
1	(3- to 4-lb.) package **cut up chicken**
1	cup **all-purpose flour**
1	Tbsp. **paprika**
2	tsp. **seasoned salt**
¼	tsp. **pepper**
¼	cup **butter** or **margarine**, melted

1. Combine first 3 ingredients in a large zip-top plastic freezer bag. Add chicken. Seal and marinate in the refrigerator at least 8 hours, turning occasionally.

2. Preheat oven to 350°.

3. Remove chicken from marinade, discarding marinade. Combine flour and next 3 ingredients in a large zip-top plastic freezer bag. Add chicken, a few pieces at a time, shaking bag to coat. Arrange chicken on a 15- x 10-inch jelly-roll pan lined with aluminum foil. Drizzle chicken with melted butter.

4. Bake at 350° for 1 hour or until golden.

Note: Dredging the chicken in Step 3 can be messy, but a couple of options make it neater. Use tongs to transfer the wet chicken to the flour mixture. Or use disposable plastic gloves designed for use in food service. The gloves are inexpensive, available at large grocery stores or discount centers, and ideal for promoting food safety.

Roasted Garlic Mashed Potatoes

makes 6 to 8 servings ☆ prep: 35 min. ☆ cook: 1 hr., 16 min.

3	large **garlic bulbs**	3	Tbsp. **olive oil**
3	lb. **baking potatoes,** cut into 3-inch pieces	¾	tsp. **salt**
3	Tbsp. **unsalted butter**	¼	tsp. ground **white pepper**
		1	cup **half-and-half**

1. Preheat oven to 350°.

2. Peel outer skins from garlic bulbs, and discard skins. Cut off and discard top one-fourth of each garlic bulb. Place garlic, cut side up, in center of a piece of heavy-duty aluminum foil; fold foil over garlic, sealing tightly. Bake at 350° for 1 hour or until garlic bulbs are soft. Remove from oven; let cool completely.

3. Squeeze pulp from garlic bulbs into a small bowl, and press with back of a spoon to make a paste. Set aside.

4. Cook potatoes in boiling water to cover 15 minutes or until tender; drain. Mash potatoes in a large bowl; stir in garlic paste, butter, and next 3 ingredients.

5. Microwave half-and-half in a microwave-safe bowl at HIGH 1 minute. Gradually stir warm half-and-half into potato mixture.

Note: Adding warmed versus cold half-and-half to the potatoes in Step 5 assures a velvety texture.

Buttery roasted garlic cloves make these creamy, rich mashed potatoes taste like heaven. For family fun, give everyone small romaine lettuce leaves to use like spoons to eat the potatoes just like the ancient Greeks.

Chicken and Dumplings

makes 4 to 6 servings ☆ prep: 15 min. ☆ cook: 25 min.

1   (32-oz.) container **low-sodium chicken broth**

1   (14½-oz.) can **low-sodium chicken broth**

3   cups shredded **cooked chicken** (about 1½ lb.)

1   (10¾-oz.) can **reduced-fat cream of celery soup**

¼   tsp. **poultry seasoning**

1   (10.2-oz.) can **refrigerated jumbo buttermilk biscuits**

Starting with refrigerated biscuits allows you to serve up this classic comfort food any day of the week.

1. Stir together first 5 ingredients in a Dutch oven over medium-high heat; bring to a boil. Reduce heat to low; simmer, stirring occasionally, 15 minutes.

2. Place biscuits on a lightly floured surface. Roll or pat each biscuit to ⅛-inch thickness; cut into ½-inch-wide strips.

3. Return broth mixture to a low boil over medium-high heat. Drop strips, 1 at a time, into boiling broth. Reduce heat to low; simmer 10 minutes, stirring occasionally to prevent dumplings from sticking.

Note: We used a deli-roasted chicken for this recipe. One chicken yields about 3 cups.

fresh addition

For a flavorful variation of this quick favorite, add 2 diced carrots and 3 diced celery ribs when adding the biscuit strips.

Chicken Cutlets with Pecan Sauce

makes 4 servings ☆ prep: 16 min. ☆ cook: 13 min.

This easy yet elegant chicken is the answer to your weeknight dinner dilemma.

½ cup chopped **pecans**
¼ cup **butter**, divided
4 **chicken cutlets** (about 1¼ lb.)
1 tsp. **salt**
½ tsp. **pepper**
3 Tbsp. **all-purpose flour**

3 Tbsp. **olive oil**
½ cup **chicken broth**
1 Tbsp. **brown sugar**
2 Tbsp. **cider vinegar**
½ tsp. **dried thyme**

1. Heat pecans and 2 Tbsp. butter in a large nonstick skillet over medium-low heat, stirring often, 2 to 3 minutes or until nuts are toasted and fragrant. Remove from skillet.

2. Sprinkle chicken with salt and pepper. Dredge in flour.

3. Cook chicken in hot oil in skillet over medium heat 3 to 4 minutes on each side or until golden brown and cooked through. Transfer to a serving platter. Top with pecans.

4. Add chicken broth to skillet, and cook 2 minutes, stirring to loosen particles from bottom of skillet. Add brown sugar, vinegar, and thyme, and cook 3 to 4 minutes or until sugar is melted and sauce is slightly thickened. Whisk in remaining 2 Tbsp. butter. Serve sauce over chicken.

simple side

Garlicky Baby Mixed Veggies: Cook 1 (11-oz.) package frozen steam-in-bag baby mixed vegetables according to package directions. Toss with 1 tsp. freshly ground garlic-pepper seasoning.

Note: We tested with Green Giant Valley Fresh Steamers Market Blend and McCormick seasoning.

Shrimp and Andouille Sausage with Asiago Grits

makes 6 servings ☆ prep: 25 min. ☆ cook: 19 min.

Andouille sausage adds a Cajun flair to this indulgent Southern staple.

1½ lb. **unpeeled, medium-size raw shrimp**
1 Tbsp. **butter**
½ lb. **andouille sausage,** diced
¾ cup **whipping cream**
⅓ cup **chicken broth**
⅓ cup **dry white wine**
½ cup freshly grated **Asiago** or **Parmesan cheese**
¼ tsp. ground **white pepper**
Asiago Grits
Garnish: chopped **fresh chives**

1. Peel shrimp; devein, if desired.

2. Melt butter in a large skillet over medium-high heat. Add sausage; cook, stirring constantly, 5 minutes or until lightly browned. Add shrimp, and cook, stirring constantly, 3 to 5 minutes or just until shrimp turn pink. Remove shrimp and sausage mixture from skillet.

3. Add cream, broth, and wine to skillet; cook over medium heat, stirring constantly, 5 minutes or until slightly thickened. Stir in cheese and pepper; cook, stirring constantly, 6 to 8 minutes or until cheese is melted. Stir in shrimp and sausage mixture. Serve over Asiago Grits. Garnish, if desired.

Asiago Grits

makes 6 servings ☆ prep: 5 min. ☆ cook: 12 min.

2 (14-oz.) cans **chicken broth**
¾ cup uncooked **quick-cooking grits**
½ (8-oz.) container **chive-and-onion cream cheese**
½ cup freshly grated **Asiago** or **Parmesan cheese**
¼ tsp. ground **white pepper**

1. Bring chicken broth to a boil in a medium saucepan over medium-high heat; gradually whisk in grits. Cover, reduce heat to medium-low, and simmer, stirring occasionally, 12 to 15 minutes or until thickened. Add cheeses and pepper, stirring until melted.

Parmesan-Pecan Fried Catfish with Pickled Okra Salsa

makes 6 servings ☆ prep: 10 min. ☆ cook: 8 min. ☆ other: 1 hr.

2	lb. **catfish fillets**, cut into 1-inch-wide strips	1	Tbsp. **Cajun seasoning**	
1	cup **buttermilk**	1	Tbsp. **paprika**	
1	cup ground **pecans**	2	large **eggs**, beaten	
⅔	cup plain **yellow cornmeal**		**Vegetable oil**	
⅔	cup grated **Parmesan cheese**		Pickled Okra Salsa	

The secret to ensuring a crispy, golden crust is maintaining an oil temperature of 350°.

1. Place catfish and buttermilk in a large zip-top plastic freezer bag. Seal and chill 1 hour. Remove catfish from buttermilk, discarding buttermilk.

2. Combine pecans and next 4 ingredients in a shallow bowl. Dip fish in eggs; dredge in pecan mixture, shaking off excess. Arrange on a baking sheet. Pour oil to depth of 1½ inches into a cast-iron Dutch oven or 12-inch (2¼-inch-deep) cast-iron skillet; heat to 350°. Fry fish, in batches, 2 to 3 minutes or until golden brown and fish flakes with a fork. Drain on a wire rack over paper towels. Serve with Pickled Okra Salsa.

Note: We tested with Zatarain's Creole Seasoning.

Pickled Okra Salsa

makes about 1½ cups ☆ prep: 10 min.

5	whole **pickled okra**, sliced	⅛	tsp. freshly ground **pepper**	
½	cup chopped **sweet onion**	1	(14.5-oz.) can **diced tomatoes with mild green chiles**, drained	
4	tsp. chopped **fresh cilantro**			
1	tsp. **fresh lime juice**			
¼	tsp. **salt**			

Store in refrigerator up to 7 days. If refrigerated, let stand at room temperature 15 minutes before serving.

1. Pulse first 6 ingredients and half of tomatoes in a food processor 4 to 6 times or until thoroughly combined. Stir in remaining diced tomatoes. Serve immediately, or cover and chill.

Sizzling Flounder

makes 4 servings ☆ prep: 10 min. ☆ cook: 25 min.

This recipe hails from Charleston, where flounder is a favorite, but any firm-fleshed fish, such as tilapia, grouper, or catfish, will do. Adjust the cooking time according to the thickness of the fish.

¼	cup grated **Parmesan cheese**	¼	tsp. **pepper**
1	tsp. **paprika**	½	cup **butter**
4	(6-oz.) **flounder fillets**	2	Tbsp. **fresh lemon juice**
¾	tsp. **salt**		

1. Place 1 oven rack 5 inches from heat; place a second rack in middle of oven. Combine Parmesan cheese and paprika. Season fish with salt and pepper.

2. Preheat oven to 450°. Heat butter in a broiler-safe 13- x 9-inch baking dish in oven 8 minutes or until butter is melted and beginning to brown. Place fish in hot butter, skin side up.

3. Bake at 450° on middle oven rack 10 minutes. Carefully flip fish, and baste with pan juices. Sprinkle with lemon juice and Parmesan cheese mixture. Bake 5 minutes more or just until fish flakes with a fork. Remove from oven; increase oven temperature to broil.

4. Broil fish on oven rack 5 inches from heat 2 to 3 minutes or until bubbly and golden brown.

serve with

Bacon-Fried Okra

makes about 4 servings ☆ prep: 15 min. ☆ cook: 10 min.

½	lb. **fresh okra**	**Salt** to taste
2	**bacon** slices	

1. Finely chop okra.

2. Cook bacon in a skillet over medium heat just until crisp; remove bacon, and set aside for other use. Reserve drippings in skillet.

3. Sauté okra in 2 Tbsp. hot bacon drippings over medium-high heat 10 to 12 minutes or until lightly browned. Sprinkle with salt to taste.

serve with

Hot Slaw à la Greyhound Grill

makes 6 servings ☆ prep: 24 min. ☆ cook: 16 min.

½   large **red cabbage** (about 1½ lb.), shredded

½   large **green cabbage** (about 1½ lb.), shredded

4   thick **bacon** slices, diced

½   cup **cider vinegar**

½   tsp. **celery seeds**

¼   tsp. **dried crushed red pepper**

2   tsp. **salt**

1   tsp. freshly ground **black pepper**

Pepper vinegar to taste (optional)

This tangy slaw is a favorite of award-winning cookbook authors Matt and Ted Lee.

1. Bring 3½ qt. water to a boil in a large stockpot. Cook shredded cabbage in boiling water 4 minutes or just until it turns a dull gray-purple. Remove from heat; drain well.

2. Cook bacon in a skillet over medium-low heat 8 minutes or just until crisp; remove bacon, and drain on paper towels, reserving drippings in skillet.

3. Stir cider vinegar, celery seeds, and red pepper into hot drippings, stirring to loosen particles from bottom of skillet. Stir in cabbage, salt, black pepper, and bacon; cook, stirring occasionally, 4 minutes or until cabbage is tender and red cabbage turns a bright magenta color. Place mixture in a serving dish, and, if desired, sprinkle with pepper vinegar to taste.

Fresh Vegetable Lasagna

makes 8 servings ☆ prep: 18 min. ☆ cook: 1 hr., 19 min. ☆ stand: 10 min.

Serve this nourishing Italian meal with garlic toast for soaking up the delicious homemade sauce. If you're in a hurry, use your favorite store-bought low-sodium marinara sauce.

4 medium **zucchini,** halved lengthwise and thinly sliced (about 1½ lb.)
1 (8-oz.) package sliced **fresh mushrooms**
2 **garlic cloves,** minced
Vegetable cooking spray
1 medium-size **red bell pepper,** chopped
1 medium-size **yellow bell pepper,** chopped
1 **yellow onion,** chopped

½ tsp. **salt**
1½ cups **fat-free ricotta cheese**
1 large **egg**
2 cups (8 oz.) shredded **part-skim mozzarella cheese,** divided
½ cup freshly grated **Parmesan cheese,** divided
5 cups Basic Marinara Sauce
1 (8-oz.) package **no-boil lasagna noodles**

1. Preheat oven to 450°. Bake zucchini, mushrooms, and garlic in a jelly-roll pan coated with cooking spray 12 to 14 minutes or until vegetables are crisp-tender, stirring halfway through. Repeat procedure with bell peppers and onion. Reduce oven temperature to 350°. Toss together vegetables and salt in a bowl.

2. Stir together ricotta, egg, 1½ cups shredded mozzarella cheese, and ¼ cup grated Parmesan cheese.

3. Spread 1 cup Basic Marinara Sauce in a 13- x 9-inch baking dish coated with cooking spray. Top with 3 noodles, 1 cup sauce, one-third of ricotta mixture, and one-third of vegetable mixture; repeat layers twice, beginning with 3 noodles. Top with remaining noodles and 1 cup sauce. Sprinkle with remaining ½ cup shredded mozzarella and ¼ cup grated Parmesan.

4. Bake, covered, at 350° for 45 minutes. Uncover and bake 10 to 15 more minutes or until cheese is melted and golden. Let stand 10 minutes.

Note: We tested with Ronzoni Oven Ready Lasagna.

Basic Marinara Sauce

makes 11 cups ☆ prep: 15 min. ☆ cook: 1 hr., 2 min.

3 cups chopped **yellow onions** (about 3 medium)
1 Tbsp. **olive oil**
1 Tbsp. **sugar**
3 **garlic cloves,** minced
5 tsp. **freshly ground Italian seasoning**

2 tsp. **salt**
2 Tbsp. **balsamic vinegar**
2 cups **low-sodium fat-free vegetable broth**
3 (28-oz.) cans **no-salt-added crushed tomatoes**

This recipe makes a big batch, so freeze the extra for a head start on another meal.

1. Sauté onions in hot oil in a large Dutch oven over medium-high heat 5 minutes or until tender. Add sugar and next 3 ingredients; sauté 1 minute. Stir in vinegar; cook 30 seconds. Add broth and tomatoes. Bring to a boil; reduce heat to low, and simmer, stirring occasionally, 55 minutes or until sauce thickens.

Note: We tested with McCormick Italian Herb Seasoning Grinder (set on medium) and Dei Fratelli Crushed Tomatoes.

make ahead

Make this sauce ahead, and store it in the refrigerator up to five days, or freeze it in smaller batches up to three months.

Three-Cheese Pasta Bake

makes 4 servings ☆ prep: 20 min. ☆ cook: 7 min. ☆ bake: 15 min.

1   (8-oz.) package **penne pasta**
2   Tbsp. **butter**
2   Tbsp. **all-purpose flour**
1½ cups **milk**
½   cup **half-and-half**
1   cup (4 oz.) shredded **white Cheddar cheese**
¼   cup grated **Parmesan cheese**
2   cups (8 oz.) shredded **Gruyère cheese,** divided
1   tsp. **salt**
¼   tsp. **pepper**
Pinch of ground **nutmeg**

Mac and cheese, the quintessential comfort food, gets a great update with penne pasta and a trio of cheeses.

1. Preheat oven to 350°. Prepare pasta according to package directions.

2. Meanwhile, melt butter in a saucepan over medium heat. Whisk in flour until smooth; cook, whisking constantly, 1 minute. Gradually whisk in milk and half-and-half; cook, whisking constantly, 3 to 5 minutes or until thickened. Stir in Cheddar cheese, Parmesan cheese, 1 cup Gruyère cheese, and next 3 ingredients until smooth.

3. Stir together pasta and cheese mixture; pour into a lightly greased 11- x 7-inch baking dish. Top with remaining 1 cup Gruyère cheese.

4. Bake, uncovered, at 350° for 15 minutes or until golden and bubbly.

make ahead

To make ahead, proceed with recipe as directed, but don't top with remaining 1 cup Gruyère cheese. Cover and chill up to 8 hours. When you're ready to enjoy it, let stand at room temperature 30 minutes. Bake at 350° for 20 to 25 minutes or until bubbly. Increase oven temperature to 400°. Top with remaining Gruyère; bake 10 more minutes or until golden.

Watermelon Salsa, page 50

Chapter 2

QUICK & EASY HOMESTYLE

Watermelon Salsa

makes about 3 cups ☆ prep: 20 min. ☆ pictured on page 48

This fast appetizer recipe doubles as a healthful and refreshing topping for grilled, baked, or broiled fish, shrimp, or chicken.

1½ tsp. **lime zest**
¼   cup **fresh lime juice** (about 3 limes)
1   Tbsp. **sugar**
¾   tsp. ground **black pepper**
3   cups seeded and finely chopped **watermelon**
1   **cucumber**, peeled, seeded, and diced

2   **jalapeño peppers**, seeded and minced
¼   cup chopped **red onion**
¼   cup chopped **fresh basil**
½   tsp. **salt**
Tortilla chips

1. Whisk together first 4 ingredients in a large bowl. Add watermelon and next 4 ingredients, tossing gently to coat. Chill until ready to serve. Stir in salt just before serving. Serve with tortilla chips.

Black-eyed-Pea-and-Ham Dip

makes 12 appetizer servings ☆ prep: 20 min. ☆ cook: 11 min.

½   cup diced **country ham**
2   (15.8-oz.) cans **black-eyed peas**, drained and rinsed
1   large **tomato**, finely chopped
2   **green onions**, sliced
1   **celery rib**, finely chopped

¼   cup chopped **fresh parsley**
2   Tbsp. **olive oil**
1   to 2 Tbsp. **apple cider vinegar**
Cornbread crackers

1. Sauté ham in a lightly greased large nonstick skillet over medium-high heat 3 to 5 minutes or until lightly browned; stir in black-eyed peas and ¾ cup water. Reduce heat to medium, and simmer 8 minutes or until liquid is reduced by three-fourths. Partially mash beans with back of a spoon to desired consistency.

2. Stir together tomato and next 5 ingredients. Spoon warm bean mixture into a serving dish, and top with tomato mixture. Serve with crackers.

Black-eyed-Pea-and-Ham Dip

Blue Cheese Ranch Dip

Blue Cheese Ranch Dip

makes 2½ cups ☆ prep: 5 min.

1   (16-oz.) container **sour cream**
1   (1-oz.) package **Ranch dip mix**
1   (4-oz.) package **blue cheese crumbles**
2 Tbsp. chopped **fresh chives**
Carrot and **celery sticks, sturdy potato chips,** and **hot wings**

1. Stir together sour cream, Ranch dip mix, blue cheese crumbles, and chopped fresh chives. Serve with carrot and celery sticks, sturdy potato chips, and hot wings.

Note: To save more time, look for precut carrot and celery sticks in the produce department.

Herb Dip

makes about 1 cup ☆ prep: 5 min.

4   oz. **goat cheese,** softened
½   cup **plain nonfat yogurt**
3   Tbsp. assorted chopped **fresh herbs**
1   **garlic clove,** minced
1   Tbsp. **lemon juice**
Salt and **pepper** to taste
Fresh cut **vegetables**

1. Process goat cheese, yogurt, chopped fresh herbs, minced garlic, and lemon juice in a food processor until smooth. Add salt and pepper to taste. Serve with fresh cut vegetables.

Spring Salad

makes 4 servings ☆ prep: 20 min. ☆ cook: 2 min.

To make your own vinaigrette, all you need is oil, vinegar, salt, pepper, and a jar with a tight-fitting lid. Balsamic vinegar and olive oil is our preferred combination, though cider vinegar, canola oil, and flavored oils such as hazelnut or walnut work well, too. Because balsamic is a sweeter-tasting vinegar, we like the ratio of 1 part vinegar to 2 parts oil. (The standard ratio for other vinegars is 1 part vinegar to 3 parts oil.) Put these in the jar with the salt and pepper; shake well, and you're done.

1   lb. fresh **asparagus**
8   cups **baby salad greens,** thoroughly washed
2   cups **seedless red grapes**
8   cooked **bacon** slices, crumbled
1   (4-oz.) package **goat cheese,** crumbled
4   **green onions,** sliced
¼   cup **pine nuts**
Balsamic vinaigrette

1. Snap off and discard tough ends of asparagus; arrange asparagus in a steamer basket over boiling water. Cover and steam 2 to 4 minutes or until asparagus is crisp-tender. Plunge asparagus into ice water to stop the cooking process; drain and cut into 1-inch pieces.

2. Arrange salad greens on a serving platter; top evenly with asparagus, grapes, and next 4 ingredients. Drizzle with vinaigrette.

Note: For this recipe, use your favorite brand of bottled balsamic vinaigrette, or make one from scratch as described at left. Home-made salad dressing is one of those small touches that makes a meal special. Best of all, in 5 minutes flat you can whisk together a batch of delicious vinaigrette that can be stored in the refrigerator for up to 5 days.

Tomato-Cucumber Salad

makes 4 servings ☆ prep: 10 min.

1   **seedless cucumber**, sliced
½   small **onion**, thinly sliced
2   cups quartered small, **vine-ripened tomatoes**
¼   cup **olive oil–and-vinegar dressing**

½   tsp. **lemon zest**
1   Tbsp. **lemon juice**
Salt and **pepper** to taste

This fresh salad is best in the summer when tomatoes and cucumbers are at their peak flavor.

1. Stir together cucumber, onion, and tomatoes. Add dressing, lemon zest, lemon juice, and salt and pepper. Toss to coat.

Note: We tested with Campari tomatoes and Newman's Own Olive Oil & Vinegar Dressing.

Beef-and-Vegetable Stir-Fry

makes 4 servings ☆ prep: 25 min. ☆ cook: 10 min.

1 lb. fresh **asparagus**
12 oz. **top round steak,** cut into thin strips
3 Tbsp. **all-purpose flour**
¼ cup **soy sauce**
2 **garlic cloves,** minced
1 Tbsp. **dark sesame oil,** divided
1 Tbsp. **hoisin sauce**
¼ tsp. **dried crushed red pepper**
4 small **carrots,** cut diagonally into ¼-inch-thick slices
1 small **red bell pepper,** cut into thin strips
½ cup sliced **fresh mushrooms**
5 **green onions,** cut into 1-inch pieces
2 cups **hot cooked rice**

Stir-fry is a great way to whip up a quick dinner and use up those leftover veggies in the back of your refrigerator. Feel free to substitute whatever you have on hand—just adjust the cooking time to ensure a tender-crisp texture.

1. Snap off tough ends of asparagus; cut spears into 1-inch pieces, and set aside.

2. Dredge steak in flour; set aside.

3. Stir together soy sauce, ¼ cup water, garlic, 1 tsp. sesame oil, hoisin sauce, and red pepper.

4. Heat remaining 2 tsp. oil in a large skillet or wok over medium-high heat 2 minutes. Add beef and carrots, and stir-fry 4 minutes. Add soy sauce mixture, and stir-fry 1 minute. Add asparagus, bell pepper, mushrooms, and green onions, and stir-fry 3 minutes. Serve over rice.

30-Minute Chili

makes 8 servings ☆ prep: 5 min. ☆ cook: 25 min.

A homemade seasoning mix gives this quick chili great taste.

2 lb. **lean ground beef**
⅓ cup Chili Seasoning Mix
2 (14.5-oz.) cans **diced tomatoes with green pepper, celery, and onion**
2 (8-oz.) cans **tomato sauce**
1 (16-oz.) can **black beans,** undrained
1 (15.5-oz.) can **small red beans,** undrained
Toppings: **corn chips,** shredded **Cheddar cheese**

1. Cook beef in a Dutch oven over medium-high heat, stirring often, 4 to 5 minutes or until beef crumbles and is no longer pink; drain well. Return beef to Dutch oven; sprinkle with seasoning mix. Cook 1 minute over medium-high heat.

2. Stir in diced tomatoes and next 3 ingredients; bring to a boil over medium-high heat, stirring occasionally. Cover, reduce heat to low, and simmer, stirring occasionally, 15 minutes. Serve with desired toppings.

Chili Seasoning Mix

makes about 1⅓ cups ☆ prep: 5 min.

This versatile mix yields big dividends in time-saving suppers. Loaded with flavor, it pairs perfectly with beef, pork, poultry, or seafood.

¾ cup **chili powder**
2 Tbsp. **ground cumin**
2 Tbsp. **dried oregano**
2 Tbsp. **dried minced onion**
2 Tbsp. **seasoned salt**
2 Tbsp. **sugar**
2 tsp. **dried minced garlic**

1. Stir together all ingredients. Store seasoning mix in an airtight container up to 4 months at room temperature. Shake or stir well before using.

Cheesy BBQ Sloppy Joes

makes 4 servings ☆ prep: 8 min. ☆ cook: 18 min.

Thick-cut, store-bought frozen Texas toast gives you a head start on this quick, hearty meal.

1½ lb. **lean ground beef**
1 (14.5-oz.) can **diced tomatoes**
1 cup **ketchup**
½ cup bottled **barbecue sauce**
1 Tbsp. **Worcestershire sauce**
2 Tbsp. chopped **pickled jalapeño peppers** (optional)

1 Tbsp. **liquid from pickled jalapeño peppers** (optional)
1 (11.25-oz.) package **frozen garlic Texas toast**
½ cup (2 oz.) shredded **sharp Cheddar cheese**

1. Brown ground beef in a large skillet over medium-high heat, stirring often, 8 to 10 minutes or until beef crumbles and is no longer pink; drain well. Return to skillet. Stir in tomatoes, next 3 ingredients, and, if desired, jalapeño peppers and liquid. Cover and cook 10 minutes.

2. Meanwhile, prepare Texas toast according to package directions. Serve beef mixture over Texas toast; sprinkle with cheese.

simple side

Mixed Green Salad: Toss together 1 (5-oz.) package mixed salad greens; 1 pt. grape tomatoes, halved; and ½ small cucumber, sliced. Drizzle with Ranch dressing.

Easy Skillet Tacos

makes 4 to 6 servings ☆ prep: 10 min. ☆ cook: 26 min. ☆ stand: 5 min.

1   lb. **ground beef**
1   small **onion,** chopped
1   tsp. **olive oil**
1   Tbsp. **chili powder**
1½   tsp. **ground cumin**
1   tsp. **salt**
1   (15-oz.) can **pinto beans,** drained and rinsed
1   (8-oz.) can **tomato sauce**

½   cup **salsa**
1½   cups (6 oz.) **shredded Cheddar cheese**
1   Tbsp. chopped **fresh cilantro**
Taco shells or **flour tortillas,** warmed
Toppings: **shredded lettuce, diced tomatoes, salsa, sour cream**

Tacos are an easy go-to on a busy weeknight because all you have to do is prepare the beef and chop the toppings, and everyone can make their own tacos.

1. Cook ground beef in a large skillet over medium-high heat, 8 to 10 minutes stirring until beef crumbles and is no longer pink. Drain well. Remove beef; wipe skillet with a paper towel.

2. Sauté onion in hot oil in same skillet over medium-high heat. Add chili powder, cumin, salt, and beef. Cook 5 to 7 minutes, stirring occasionally. Stir in beans, tomato sauce, ¾ cup water, and salsa. Mash pinto beans in skillet with a fork, leaving some beans whole. Bring to a boil; reduce heat, and simmer, uncovered, 8 to 10 minutes or until liquid is reduced.

3. Top with cheese and cilantro. Cover, turn off heat, and let stand 5 minutes or until cheese melts. Serve with taco shells or tortillas and desired toppings.

Barbecued Pork Quesadillas

makes 4 servings ☆ prep: 10 min. ☆ cook: 16 min.

These tasty quesadillas combine Southern barbecue and Mexican cuisine into one fast and fabulous meal. Serve with grilled corn on the cob for a complete dinner.

1 lb. chopped **barbecued pork** (without sauce)

1 cup **barbecue sauce**

½ cup chopped **fresh cilantro**

2 **green onions,** minced

8 (6-inch) fajita-size **flour tortillas**

1 (8-oz.) package shredded **Mexican four-cheese blend**

Toppings: **sour cream, sliced green onions, barbecue sauce**

1. Stir together barbecued pork and next 3 ingredients.

2. Place 1 tortilla in a hot, lightly greased skillet or on a griddle. Sprinkle tortilla with ¼ cup cheese, and spoon ⅓ cup pork mixture on half of tortilla. Cook 2 to 3 minutes or until cheese melts. Fold tortilla in half over filling; transfer to a serving plate. Repeat procedure with remaining tortillas, cheese, and pork mixture. Serve with desired toppings.

Hot Sesame Pork on Mixed Greens

makes 8 servings ☆ prep: 19 min. ☆ cook: 14 min.

½ (16-oz.) package **won ton wrappers**
2 lb. **boneless pork loin**, trimmed
¾ cup **sesame seeds**, divided
1 cup **vegetable oil**, divided
½ cup **all-purpose flour**
1 tsp. **salt**
½ tsp. **pepper**
¼ cup **dark sesame oil**
½ cup firmly packed **brown sugar**
⅓ cup **soy sauce**
¼ cup **rice vinegar**
10 to 12 small **green onions**, sliced
2 (5-oz.) packages **mixed salad greens**
1 **bok choy**, shredded

Enjoy Asian flavors at home faster than you can order take-out. Frying the pork in sesame oil adds additional flavor, but you can use vegetable oil instead if desired.

1. Cut won ton wrappers into ½-inch strips, and cut pork into 3- x 1-inch strips; set aside.

2. Toast ½ cup sesame seeds in a large heavy skillet over medium-high heat, stirring constantly, 2 to 3 minutes; remove from skillet.

3. Pour ½ cup vegetable oil into skillet; heat to 375°. Fry won ton strips in batches 30 seconds or until golden. Drain on paper towels; set aside. Drain skillet.

4. Combine remaining ¼ cup sesame seeds, flour, salt, and pepper in a zip-top plastic freezer bag; add pork. Seal and shake to coat.

5. Pour 2 Tbsp. sesame oil into skillet; place over medium heat. Fry half of pork in hot oil, stirring often, 6 to 8 minutes or until golden. Remove and keep warm. Repeat procedure with remaining 2 Tbsp. sesame oil and pork.

6. Process toasted sesame seeds, remaining ½ cup vegetable oil, ½ cup brown sugar, soy sauce, and vinegar in a blender 1 to 2 minutes or until smooth.

7. Combine pork and green onions; drizzle with soy sauce mixture, tossing gently.

8. Combine mixed greens and bok choy; top with pork mixture and fried won ton strips. Serve immediately.

Chicken-and-Rice Casserole

makes 8 servings ☆ prep: 20 min. ☆ cook: 25 min.

2 Tbsp. **butter**
1 medium **onion**, chopped
1 (8.8-oz.) package **microwaveable rice** of choice
3 cups chopped **cooked chicken**
1½ cups frozen **petite peas**
1½ cups (6 oz.) shredded **sharp Cheddar cheese**
1 cup **mayonnaise**
1 (10¾-oz.) can **cream of chicken soup**
1 (8-oz.) can sliced **water chestnuts**, drained
1 (4-oz.) jar sliced **pimientos**, drained
3 cups coarsely crushed **ridged potato chips**

The potato chip topping promises to be a hit.

1. Preheat oven to 350°. Melt butter in a skillet over medium heat. Add onion, and sauté 5 minutes or until tender.

2. Cook rice in microwave according to package directions. Combine sautéed onion, rice, chicken, and next 6 ingredients in a large bowl; toss gently. Spoon mixture into a lightly greased 13- x 9-inch baking dish. Top with coarsely crushed potato chips.

3. Bake, uncovered, at 350° for 20 to 25 minutes or until bubbly.

Note: Use a rotisserie chicken for this family-friendly casserole; note that a 2-lb. chicken provides 3 cups of chicken.

make ahead

To make casserole ahead, prepare and spoon casserole into baking dish, leaving off crushed chips. Cover and refrigerate up to 24 hours. Uncover and add crushed chips before baking.

Peanut Chicken Pitas

makes 8 servings ☆ prep: 15 min.

This Asian spin on classic chicken salad is the perfect quick and easy light meal.

1   **romaine lettuce heart,** chopped

1¼   cups chopped **cooked chicken breast**

¾   cup frozen **snow peas,** thawed and trimmed

¼   cup shredded **carrot**

¼   cup chopped roasted lightly **salted peanuts**

½   cup light **sesame-ginger dressing**

8   (1-oz.) mini **whole wheat pita rounds,** halved

1. Combine chopped lettuce and next 4 ingredients in a large bowl. Drizzle with sesame-ginger dressing; toss to combine. Fill each pita half evenly with mixture.

Note: We tested with Newman's Own Low Fat Sesame Ginger Dressing and Toufayan Bakeries Hearth Baked Whole Wheat Pitettes Pita Bread.

Chicken Enchiladas

makes 4 servings ☆ prep: 15 min. ☆ cook: 30 min.

3 cups chopped **cooked chicken**

2 cups (8 oz.) shredded **pepper Jack cheese**

½ cup **sour cream**

1 (4.5-oz.) can chopped **green chiles,** drained

⅓ cup chopped **fresh cilantro**

8 (8-inch) **flour tortillas**

Vegetable cooking spray

1 (8-oz.) container **sour cream**

1 (8-oz.) jar **tomatillo salsa**

Toppings: **diced tomatoes, chopped avocado, chopped green onions, sliced ripe olives**

Substitute leftover roast beef or your favorite shredded barbecued pork as a tasty alternative to chicken.

1. Preheat oven to 350°. Stir together first 5 ingredients. Spoon chicken mixture evenly down center of each tortilla, and roll up. Arrange seam side down in a lightly greased 13- x 9-inch baking dish.

2. Coat tortillas with cooking spray.

3. Bake at 350° for 30 minutes or until golden brown.

4. Stir together 8-oz. container sour cream and salsa. Spoon over hot enchiladas; sprinkle with desired toppings.

Tangy Turkey Burgers

makes 6 servings ☆ prep: 15 min. ☆ cook: 12 min.

These flavorful burgers get their tang from a prepared chicken marinade.

1½ lb. **ground turkey**
2 **green onions,** chopped
2 Tbsp. **white wine–and-herb chicken marinade**
1 tsp. **garlic salt with parsley**
1 tsp. **pepper**

6 French **hamburger buns,** toasted
Toppings: **gourmet mixed lettuce leaves, sliced avocado, mayonnaise**

1. Gently combine first 5 ingredients. Shape mixture into 6 (4-inch) patties.

2. Heat a cast-iron grill pan over medium-high heat. Cook patties in pan 6 to 8 minutes on each side or until done. Serve burgers on buns with desired toppings.

Note: We tested with Publix French Hamburger Buns, McCormick California Style Garlic Salt with Parsley, and Lea & Perrins Marinade for Chicken.

simple side

Sesame Sweet Potato Fries: Toss 1 (20-oz.) package frozen sweet potato fries with 1 Tbsp. sesame seeds, 1 Tbsp. sesame oil, and 1 tsp. kosher salt. Bake according to package directions.

Linguine with Sun-Dried Tomatoes

makes 6 servings ☆ prep: 16 min. ☆ cook: 10 min.

Sun-dried tomatoes contribute a rich depth of flavor when fresh tomatoes are out of season.

1 (16-oz.) package linguine
1 (7-oz.) jar sun-dried tomatoes in oil
¼ cup pine nuts
3 garlic cloves, minced
¼ cup extra-virgin olive oil
1 (4-oz.) package crumbled feta cheese
2 Tbsp. thin fresh basil strips

1. Prepare linguine according to package directions.

2. Drain tomatoes, reserving 2 Tbsp. oil. Cut tomatoes into thin strips.

3. Heat pine nuts in a large nonstick skillet over medium-low heat, stirring often, 5 minutes or until toasted and fragrant. Remove nuts from skillet.

4. Increase heat to medium, and sauté garlic in 2 Tbsp. reserved oil and olive oil in skillet 1 minute or until garlic is fragrant. Stir in tomatoes, and remove from heat.

5. Toss together tomato mixture, hot cooked pasta, feta cheese, and basil in a large bowl. Sprinkle with toasted pine nuts.

variation

Linguine with Tuna and Sun-Dried Tomatoes: Prepare recipe as directed. Stir in 2 (6-oz.) aluminum foil pouches solid white tuna chunks, drained, and 1 (3-oz.) can sliced black olives, drained.

Pimiento Cheese Panini

makes 10 servings ☆ prep: 15 min. ☆ cook: 3 min. per batch

¾ cup **mayonnaise**
1 (4-oz.) jar **diced pimiento,** drained
1 tsp. **Worcestershire sauce**
1 tsp. finely grated **onion**
¼ tsp. **ground red pepper**
1 (8-oz.) block **extra-sharp Cheddar cheese,** finely shredded

1 (8-oz.) block **sharp Cheddar cheese,** shredded
2 medium **jalapeño peppers,** seeded and minced (optional)
2 (16-oz.) loaves **ciabatta bread**
Olive oil

It's tough to deny the simple pleasure of this classic cheese spread, especially when it's slathered onto crusty peasant bread and then grilled. These melt-in-your-mouth sandwiches pair perfectly with a bowl of tomato soup.

1. Stir together first 5 ingredients in a large bowl; stir in cheeses and, if desired, jalapeño.

2. Slice bread into 20 (½-inch-thick) diagonal slices. Spread half of slices with pimiento cheese. Top with remaining slices. Brush outside of bread slices with olive oil.

3. Preheat panini press. Grill sandwiches, in batches, 3 to 4 minutes or until golden brown and cheese is melted. Cut sandwiches in half, if desired.

make ahead

Make pimiento cheese up to 1 week ahead and store in refrigerator.

Homemade Applesauce

makes about 6 cups ☆ prep: 20 min. ☆ cook: 20 min.

For the best taste and texture, use a variety of apples—such as Granny Smith, Golden Delicious, and Gala—when making apple-sauce and apple pie. Stir in a little chopped rosemary, and serve this applesauce as a side dish with pork chops or hash browns.

12	large **apples,** peeled and coarsely chopped	1	cup **sugar**
		½	**lemon,** sliced

1. Cook all ingredients in a Dutch oven over medium heat, stir-ring often, 20 minutes or until apples are tender and juices are thickened. Remove and discard lemon slices. Serve applesauce warm, or let cool and store in an airtight container in the refrigerator for up to 1 week.

variation

Spiced Applesauce: Substitute ½ cup firmly packed brown sugar and ½ cup granulated sugar for 1 cup sugar. Omit lemon slices, and add 1 tsp. ground cinnamon and ¼ tsp. ground cloves; prepare as directed.

Sweet Corn and Zucchini

makes 4 to 6 servings ☆ prep: 20 min. ☆ cook: 10 min.

2   cups coarsely chopped
    zucchini
½   cup diced **sweet onion**
3   Tbsp. **butter**

2   cups **fresh corn kernels**
¼   cup chopped **fresh chives**
2   tsp. **taco seasoning mix**

The taco seasoning mix adds a burst of flavor to this crisp, colorful vegetable medley.

1. Sauté zucchini and onion in butter in a large skillet over medium-high heat 5 minutes. Add corn kernels, chives, and taco seasoning mix; sauté 5 minutes or until tender.

Crunchy Fried Okra

makes 4 to 6 servings ☆ prep: 20 min. ☆ cook: 6 min.

Whole okra, halved lengthwise, gives a fun twist to this fried favorite.

Peanut oil
1½ cups **buttermilk**
1 large **egg**
2 cups **saltine cracker crumbs**
(2 sleeves)

1½ cups **all-purpose flour**
1 tsp. **salt**
1 lb. **fresh okra**, cut in half
lengthwise
Salt (optional)

1. Pour oil to a depth of 2 inches into a Dutch oven or cast-iron skillet; heat to 375°.

2. Stir together buttermilk and egg. Combine cracker crumbs, flour, and salt. Dip okra pieces in buttermilk mixture; dredge in cracker crumb mixture.

3. Fry okra, in 3 batches, 2 minutes or until golden, turning once. Drain on paper towels. Sprinkle lightly with salt, if desired.

Green Peas with Crispy Bacon

makes 12 servings ☆ prep: 20 min. ☆ cook: 17 min.

4	**bacon** slices		½	tsp. **salt**
2	**shallots,** sliced		2	(16-oz.) packages **frozen sweet peas,** thawed*
1	tsp. **orange zest**			
1	cup **fresh orange juice**		2	to 3 Tbsp. chopped **fresh mint**
1	tsp. **pepper**		1	Tbsp. **butter**

Mint and orange brighten the flavor of this simple side dish. Early in the season, while you can, use fresh peas.

1. Cook bacon in a large skillet over medium heat until crisp. Remove and crumble bacon; reserve 2 tsp. drippings in skillet.

2. Sauté shallots in hot drippings over medium-high heat 2 minutes or until tender. Stir in orange zest, orange juice, pepper, and salt. Cook, stirring occasionally, 5 minutes or until reduced by half. Add peas, and cook 5 minutes; stir in mint and butter.

3. Transfer peas to a serving dish, and sprinkle with crumbled bacon.

*6 cups shelled fresh sweet peas may be substituted. Cook peas in boiling water to cover 5 minutes; drain and proceed with recipe as directed.

Feta-Stuffed Tomatoes

makes 8 servings ☆ prep: 15 min. ☆ cook: 15 min.

4	large **tomatoes**		2	Tbsp. **olive oil**
4	oz. crumbled **feta cheese**		¼	tsp. **salt**
¼	cup fine, dry **breadcrumbs**		¼	tsp. **pepper**
2	Tbsp. chopped **green onions**			Garnish: **fresh flat-leaf parsley**
2	Tbsp. chopped **fresh flat-leaf parsley**			

1. Preheat oven to 350°. Cut tomatoes in half horizontally. Scoop out pulp from each tomato half, leaving shells intact; discard seeds, and coarsely chop pulp.

2. Stir together pulp, feta cheese, and next 6 ingredients in a bowl. Spoon mixture into tomato shells, and place in a 13- x 9-inch baking dish.

3. Bake at 350° for 15 minutes. Garnish, if desired.

Brussels Sprouts with Pancetta

makes 8 servings ☆ prep: 10 min. ☆ cook: 17 min.

2   lb. fresh **Brussels sprouts,** trimmed and halved
2   Tbsp. **olive oil**
¼   tsp. **salt**

¼   tsp. **pepper**
6   (⅛-inch-thick) **pancetta** slices
1   Tbsp. freshly grated **Parmesan cheese**

1. Preheat oven to 425°. Toss together Brussels sprouts and next 3 ingredients in a 15- x 10-inch jelly-roll pan. Bake 17 to 20 minutes or until sprouts are tender and edges are lightly browned, stirring occasionally.

2. Meanwhile, cook pancetta in a large skillet over medium heat 8 to 10 minutes or until crisp. Remove pancetta, and drain on paper towels. Crumble pancetta.

3. Remove sprouts from oven, and place in a large serving dish. Top with cheese and crumbled pancetta.

Buttery Dijon Deviled Eggs, page 88

Chapter 3

CASUAL
ENTERTAINING

Buttery Dijon Deviled Eggs

makes 2 dozen ☆ prep: 15 min. ☆ chill: 1 hr. ☆ pictured on page 86

Prepare this recipe as an appetizer or side dish, and refrigerate up to 2 days in advance.

1   dozen large **hard-cooked eggs,** peeled
¼   cup **butter,** softened
¼   cup **mayonnaise**
1   Tbsp. **Dijon mustard**

1   tsp. **fresh lemon juice**
¼   tsp. **ground red pepper**
Salt to taste
Ground **white pepper** to taste
Paprika (optional)

1. Slice eggs in half lengthwise; carefully remove yolks, keeping egg white halves intact. Mash yolks; stir in butter and next 4 ingredients. Stir in salt and white pepper to taste. Spoon or pipe yolk mixture evenly into egg white halves. Sprinkle with paprika, if desired. Cover and chill at least 1 hour or until ready to serve.

serving suggestion

With deviled eggs a mainstay of Southern picnics and parties, by the 1940s every household seemed to have an indented dish just to serve them. If you don't have a deviled egg tray, place the eggs in colorful cupcake liners to prevent sliding, and arrange on a serving tray.

Stuffed Mushrooms with Pecans

makes 8 appetizer servings ☆ prep: 10 min. ☆ cook: 28 min.

2	medium **leeks**	2	Tbsp. **olive oil**	
1	(16-oz.) package fresh **mushrooms** (about 24 medium-size mushrooms)	½	cup grated **Parmesan cheese,** divided	
1	tsp. **salt,** divided	¼	cup fine, dry **breadcrumbs**	
2	**shallots,** minced	¼	cup **pecans,** chopped	
2	**garlic cloves,** minced	2	Tbsp. chopped **fresh basil**	
		Garnish: **fresh basil sprigs**		

Use mushrooms of equal size for even cooking.

1. Preheat oven to 350°. Remove and discard root ends and dark green tops of leeks. Thinly slice leeks, and rinse thoroughly under cold running water to remove grit and sand.

2. Rinse mushrooms; pat dry. Remove and discard stems. Place mushrooms, upside down, on a wire rack in an aluminum foil-lined jelly-roll pan. Sprinkle with ½ tsp. salt; invert mushrooms.

3. Bake at 350° for 15 minutes.

4. Sauté leeks, shallots, and garlic in hot oil in a large skillet over medium heat 3 to 5 minutes or until tender. Transfer mixture to a large bowl. Stir in ¼ cup Parmesan cheese, next 3 ingredients, and remaining ½ tsp. salt until well combined. Spoon 1 heaping teaspoonful leek mixture into each mushroom cap. Sprinkle with remaining ¼ cup Parmesan cheese. Bake at 350° for 10 minutes or until golden. Garnish, if desired.

Bacon-Grits Fritters

makes about 32 ☆ prep: 35 min. ☆ chill: 4 hr. ☆ cook: 3 min. per batch

To make ahead: Prepare recipe as directed through Step 2. Cover and chill in a single layer up to 4 hours. Fry as directed. You may also prepare through Step 2 and freeze on a baking sheet for 30 minutes or until firm. Transfer to a zip-top plastic bag, and freeze. Cook frozen fritters as directed in Step 3, increasing cooking time to 5 to 6 minutes or until golden and centers are thoroughly heated.

1 cup uncooked **quick-cooking grits**
4 cups **milk**
1 tsp. **salt**
1½ cups (6 oz.) shredded **extra-sharp white Cheddar cheese**
½ cup cooked and finely crumbled **bacon** (about 8 slices)
2 **green onions,** minced
½ tsp. freshly ground **pepper**
2 large **eggs**
3 cups **Japanese breadcrumbs** (panko)
Vegetable oil

1. Prepare grits according to package directions, using 4 cups milk and 1 tsp. salt. Remove from heat, and let stand 5 minutes. Stir in cheese and next 3 ingredients, stirring until cheese is melted. Spoon mixture into a lightly greased 8-inch square baking dish or pan, and chill 4 to 24 hours.

2. Roll grits into 1½-inch balls. Whisk together eggs and ¼ cup water. Dip balls in egg wash, and roll in breadcrumbs.

3. Pour oil to depth of 3 inches in a large heavy skillet; heat over medium-high heat to 350°. Fry fritters, in batches, 3 to 4 minutes or until golden brown. Drain on paper towels. Keep fritters warm on a wire rack in a pan in a 225° oven up to 30 minutes. Serve warm.

Chicken Poppers

makes 8 to 10 appetizer servings ☆ prep: 30 min. ☆ cook: 4 min. per batch

20	**vanilla wafers,** finely crushed
1½	tsp. **seasoned salt**
¾	tsp. **ground red pepper**
½	tsp. **black pepper**
1⅓	cups **all-purpose flour,** divided
¼	cup **milk**
1	large **egg**
6	**skinned and boned chicken breasts,** cut into 1½-inch pieces
1	cup **canola** or **vegetable oil**
	Ranch dressing

Tasty Chicken Poppers will make perfect traveling companions for your next picnic.

1. Stir together first 4 ingredients and 1 cup flour. Stir together milk and egg.

2. Dredge chicken pieces in remaining ⅓ cup flour. Dip in egg mixture; dredge in wafer mixture.

3. Pour oil in a large skillet; heat to 375°. Fry chicken pieces, in 4 batches, 2 to 3 minutes on each side or until done. Drain chicken on paper towels, and serve with Ranch dressing. Garnish, if desired.

Sausage, Bean, and Spinach Dip

makes about 6 cups ☆ prep: 25 min. ☆ cook: 33 min.

1 **sweet onion,** diced
1 **red bell pepper,** diced
1 (1-lb.) package **ground hot pork sausage**
2 **garlic cloves,** minced
1 tsp. chopped **fresh thyme**
½ cup **dry white wine**
1 (8-oz.) package **cream cheese,** softened
1 (6-oz.) package **fresh baby spinach,** coarsely chopped
¼ tsp. **salt**
1 (15-oz.) can **pinto beans,** drained and rinsed
½ cup (2 oz.) shredded **Parmesan cheese**
Serve with: **corn chip scoops, red bell pepper strips, pretzel rods**

This warm, hearty dip is the perfect snack to munch on while watching the game.

1. Preheat oven to 375°. Cook diced onion and next 2 ingredients in a large skillet over medium-high heat, stirring often, 8 to 10 minutes or until meat crumbles and is no longer pink. Drain. Stir in garlic and thyme; cook 1 minute. Stir in wine; cook 2 minutes or until liquid has almost completely evaporated.

2. Add cream cheese, and cook, stirring constantly, 2 minutes or until cream cheese is melted. Stir in spinach and salt, and cook, stirring constantly, 2 minutes or until spinach is wilted. Gently stir in beans. Pour mixture into a 2-qt. baking dish; sprinkle with Parmesan cheese.

3. Bake at 375° for 18 to 20 minutes or until golden brown. Serve with corn chip scoops, bell pepper strips, and pretzel rods.

Tex-Mex Egg Rolls with Creamy Cilantro Dipping Sauce

makes 28 egg rolls ☆ prep: 40 min. ☆ cook: 2 min. per batch

This fun spin on classic egg rolls is full of South-of-the-Border flavor.

1 (5-oz.) package **yellow rice**
1 tsp. **salt**
1 lb. ground **hot pork sausage**
1 (15-oz.) can **black beans**, drained and rinsed
1 (14.5-oz.) can **Mexican-style diced tomatoes**, undrained
2 cups (8 oz.) shredded **Monterey Jack cheese**
6 **green onions**, finely chopped
1 (1.25-oz.) package **taco seasoning mix**
28 **egg roll wrappers**
1 large **egg**, lightly beaten
4 cups **peanut oil**
Creamy Cilantro Dipping Sauce
Garnish: **fresh cilantro sprigs**

1. Cook rice according to package directions, using 1 tsp. salt. Cool completely.

2. Cook sausage in a skillet over medium heat 8 to 10 minutes, stirring until it crumbles and is no longer pink; drain well. Let cool.

3. Stir together rice, sausage, black beans, and next 4 ingredients in a large bowl. Spoon about ⅓ cup rice mixture in center of each egg roll wrapper.

4. Fold top corner of wrapper over filling, tucking tip of corner under filling; fold left and right corners over filling. Lightly brush remaining corner with egg; tightly roll filled end toward the remaining corner, and press gently to seal.

5. Pour oil into a heavy Dutch oven; heat to 375°. Fry egg rolls, in batches, 2 to 3 minutes or until golden. Drain on wire rack over paper towels. Serve with Creamy Cilantro Dipping Sauce. Garnish, if desired.

Creamy Cilantro Dipping Sauce

makes 3 cups ☆ prep: 10 min.

2 (10-oz.) cans **Mexican-style diced tomatoes**
1 (8-oz.) package **cream cheese,** softened

2 cups loosely packed **fresh cilantro leaves** (about 1 bunch)
1 cup **sour cream**
3 **garlic cloves,** minced

1. Process all ingredients in a food processor until smooth.

For a beautiful presentation, cut top from 1 large red bell pepper, reserving top; remove and discard seeds and membrane, leaving pepper intact. Place bell pepper on a serving plate, and fill with sauce.

Pork Tenderloin on Cornmeal Biscuits

makes 24 servings ☆ prep: 5 min. ☆ cook: 25 min. ☆ stand: 15 min.

Let guests make their own—serve sliced pork on a platter with chutney and biscuits on the side.

4 (¾- to 1-lb.) **pork tenderloins**
2 tsp. **salt**
2 tsp. ground **black pepper**
2 Tbsp. **olive oil**

Cornmeal Biscuits, halved
Texas Cranberry Chutney
Garnish: sliced **green onions**

1. Preheat oven to broil. Place pork in a lightly greased 15- x 10-inch jelly-roll pan; sprinkle with salt and pepper. Rub evenly with oil.

2. Broil 5½ inches from heat 5 minutes; reduce oven temperature to 450°, and bake 20 minutes or until a meat thermometer inserted into thickest portion registers 160°. Let stand 15 minutes before slicing. Cut into ¼-inch-thick slices (about 18 slices each).

3. Place pork slices evenly over Cornmeal Biscuit halves, and top evenly with Texas Cranberry Chutney. Garnish, if desired.

Cornmeal Biscuits

makes about 3 dozen ☆ prep: 20 min. ☆ cook: 13 min.

4	cups **self-rising flour**	2	cups **buttermilk**
½	cup **yellow cornmeal***	¼	cup **milk**
1	cup **butter,** cut up		

Perfect party fare, these mini sandwich appetizers are hearty enough to serve as a main dish.

1. Preheat oven to 425°. Combine flour and cornmeal in a large bowl; cut in butter with a pastry blender or fork until crumbly. Add buttermilk, stirring just until dry ingredients are moistened.

2. Turn dough out onto a lightly floured surface; knead 2 to 3 times. Pat or roll dough to a ½-inch thickness, and cut with a 2-inch round cutter. Place on lightly greased baking sheets. Reroll remaining dough, and proceed as directed. Brush tops with milk.

3. Bake at 425° for 13 to 15 minutes or until golden.

* White cornmeal may be substituted.

Note: The butter needs to be cut into the flour evenly and finely, almost until you can't see any bits of butter. Large pieces of butter will melt and leak out of the biscuits.

Texas Cranberry Chutney

makes 3 cups ☆ prep: 5 min. ☆ cook: 5 min.

2	(8-oz.) cans **crushed pineapple**	¼	tsp. **salt**
1	(16-oz.) can **whole-berry cranberry sauce**	1	to 2 **jalapeño peppers,** seeded and minced
¼	cup firmly packed **brown sugar**	3	**green onions,** chopped
½	tsp. ground **ginger**		

1. Drain pineapple well; pat dry with paper towels.

2. Stir together pineapple and next 4 ingredients in a small saucepan over medium heat, and bring to a boil. Reduce heat to low, and simmer, stirring often, 5 minutes or until thickened. Remove from heat, and stir in jalapeño and green onions. Cover and chill until ready to serve.

Flank Steak Sandwiches with Blue Cheese

makes 6 servings ☆ prep: 20 min. ☆ cook: 15 min.

Fire up the grill and invite the neighbors over for a casual backyard get-together.

2 large **sweet onions**
4 Tbsp. **olive oil,** divided
½ tsp. **salt,** divided
½ tsp. freshly ground **pepper,** divided
3 **red bell peppers**
6 (2- to 3-oz.) **ciabatta or deli rolls,** split
5 oz. soft ripened **blue cheese**
1½ cups loosely packed **arugula**
    Herb-Marinated Flank Steak
6 Tbsp. **mayonnaise**

1. Preheat grill to high heat (400° to 450°). Cut onions into ¼-inch-thick slices. Brush with 1 Tbsp. olive oil, and sprinkle with ¼ tsp. salt and ¼ tsp. pepper. Cut bell peppers into 1-inch-wide strips. Place pepper strips in a large bowl, and drizzle with 1 Tbsp. olive oil. Sprinkle with remaining ¼ tsp. salt and ¼ tsp. pepper; toss to coat.

2. Grill onion and bell pepper strips, covered with grill lid, 7 to 10 minutes on each side or until lightly charred and tender.

3. Brush cut sides of rolls with remaining 2 Tbsp. olive oil, and grill, cut sides down, without grill lid, 1 to 2 minutes or until lightly browned and toasted.

4. Spread blue cheese on cut sides of roll bottoms; top with arugula, bell pepper strips, steak, and onion. Spread mayonnaise on cut sides of roll tops. Place roll tops, mayonnaise sides down, on top of onion, pressing lightly.

Herb-Marinated Flank Steak

makes 6 servings ☆ prep: 15 min. ☆ chill: 30 min.
cook: 18 min. ☆ stand: 10 min.

½   small **sweet onion,** minced

3   **garlic cloves,** minced

¼   cup **olive oil**

2   Tbsp. chopped **fresh basil**

1   Tbsp. chopped **fresh thyme**

1   Tbsp. chopped **fresh rosemary**

1   tsp. **salt**

½   tsp. **dried crushed red pepper**

1¾   lb. **flank steak**

1   **lemon,** halved

1. Place first 8 ingredients in a 2-gal. zip-top plastic bag, and squeeze bag to combine. Add steak; seal bag, and chill 30 minutes to 1 hour and 30 minutes. Remove steak from marinade, discarding marinade.

2. Preheat grill to high heat (400° to 450°). Grill steak, covered with grill lid, 9 minutes on each side or to desired degree of doneness. Remove from grill; squeeze juice from lemon over steak. Let stand 10 minutes. Cut across the grain into thin slices.

Sweet-Mustard Baked Ham

makes 8 to 10 servings ☆ prep: 20 min. ☆ cook: 3 hr. ☆ stand: 20 min.

Choose the size ham that best suits your family. Bake it 20 minutes per pound and 20 minutes more once you add the second layer of glaze.

1   (8-lb.) smoked, ready-to-cook, bone-in ham
1   cup firmly packed **light brown sugar**
2   Tbsp. **cola soft drink**
1   Tbsp. **yellow mustard**
Garnish: **fresh sage sprigs**

1. Preheat oven to 350°. If necessary, trim skin or excess fat from ham. Stir together brown sugar and next 2 ingredients in a small bowl. Brush half of glaze over ham. Wrap ham tightly in heavy-duty aluminum foil. Place in a foil-lined 13- x 9-inch pan.

2. Bake ham at 350° for 2 hours and 40 minutes or until a meat thermometer inserted into ham registers 148°. Uncover ham and brush with remaining glaze. Bake, uncovered, 20 to 30 minutes or until lightly browned. Transfer to a serving dish; let stand 20 minutes. Skim fat from pan drippings, and serve drippings with ham. Garnish, if desired.

"Big Easy" Gumbo with Hoppin' John

makes 8 to 10 servings ☆ prep: 18 min. ☆ cook: 33 min.

Adding flour to hot oil creates a fast and flavorful roux. Serve this party favorite with a fresh green salad tossed with your favorite vinaigrette.

½ cup **peanut oil**
½ cup **all-purpose flour**
1 cup chopped **sweet onion**
1 cup chopped **green bell pepper**
1 cup chopped **celery**
2 tsp. **Creole seasoning**
2 tsp. minced **garlic**
3 (14-oz.) cans low-sodium **chicken broth**

4 cups shredded **cooked chicken**
½ lb. **andouille sausage,** cut into ¼-inch-thick slices
1½ cups frozen **black-eyed peas,** thawed
1 lb. peeled, **large raw shrimp** (16/20 count)
Hoppin' John

1. Heat oil in a large Dutch oven over medium-high heat; gradually whisk in flour, and cook, whisking constantly, 5 to 7 minutes or until flour is chocolate-colored. (Do not burn mixture.)

2. Reduce heat to medium. Stir in onion and next 4 ingredients, and cook, stirring constantly, 3 minutes. Gradually stir in chicken broth; add chicken and next 2 ingredients. Increase heat to medium-high, and bring to a boil. Reduce heat to low, and simmer, stirring occasionally, 20 minutes. Add shrimp, and cook 5 minutes or just until shrimp turn pink. Serve over Hoppin' John.

test kitchen tip

Gumbo that's quick to fix calls for our 10-minute method of making a roux. Be sure to use peanut oil. It's less likely to burn at the medium-high temperature needed to make a fast roux.

Hoppin' John

makes 3 cups ☆ prep: 15 min. ☆ cook: 10 min.

1 cup diced **sweet onion**
2 Tbsp. **bacon drippings**
1 (8.5-oz.) package
  ready-to-serve jasmine rice

2 cups cooked and drained
  black-eyed peas
Salt and **pepper**

1. Sauté diced onion in bacon drippings in a large skillet over medium-high heat 5 minutes or until golden.

2. Stir in rice and black-eyed peas; cook, stirring gently, 5 minutes or until thoroughly heated. Add salt and pepper to taste.

Grilled Chicken with White Barbecue Sauce

makes 5 servings ☆ prep: 15 min. ☆ chill: 4 hr. ☆ cook: 16 min.

1	Tbsp. **dried thyme**	½	tsp. **salt**
1	Tbsp. **dried oregano**	½	tsp. **pepper**
1	Tbsp. **ground cumin**	10	**chicken thighs** (about 3 lb.)*
1	Tbsp. **paprika**		**White Barbecue Sauce**
1	tsp. **onion powder**		

This versatile sauce also makes a delicious topping for baked potatoes or burgers.

1. Combine first 7 ingredients. Rinse chicken, and pat dry; rub mixture evenly over chicken. Place chicken in a zip-top plastic freezer bag. Seal and chill 4 hours. Remove chicken from bag, discarding bag.

2. Preheat grill to medium-high heat (350° to 400°). Grill, covered with grill lid, 8 to 10 minutes on each side or until a meat thermometer inserted into thickest portion registers 170°. Serve with White Barbecue Sauce.

* 4 chicken leg quarters (about 3 lb.) may be substituted for chicken thighs. Increase cooking time to 20 to 25 minutes on each side.

White Barbecue Sauce

makes 1¾ cups ☆ prep: 10 min. ☆ chill: 2 hr.

1½	cups **mayonnaise**	1	Tbsp. **spicy brown mustard**
¼	cup **white wine vinegar**	1	tsp. **sugar**
1	**garlic clove,** minced	1	tsp. **salt**
1	Tbsp. coarsely ground **pepper**	2	tsp. **horseradish**

1. Stir together all ingredients until well blended. Chill at least 2 hours before serving; store in an airtight container in refrigerator up to 1 week.

Bourbon-Cranberry Turkey Tenderloin

makes 8 to 10 servings ☆ prep: 15 min. ☆ cook: 30 min. ☆ stand: 1 hr., 15 min.

This recipe proves that turkey's not just for Thanksgiving.

1	(16-oz.) can **whole-berry cranberry sauce**	4	lb. **turkey tenderloins**
⅓	cup firmly packed **brown sugar**	1½	tsp. **salt**
⅔	cup **bourbon**	1	Tbsp. coarsely ground **pepper**
2	Tbsp. **orange zest**		Garnish: **grilled orange slices**

1. Preheat grill to medium-high heat (350° to 400°). Bring first 4 ingredients to a boil in a saucepan over medium-high heat; reduce heat to medium-low, and simmer 10 minutes or until mixture thickens slightly. Remove from heat, and let stand 30 minutes or to room temperature. Remove ½ cup cranberry mixture; reserve remaining mixture.

2. Rinse tenderloins, and pat dry with paper towels. Brush with ¼ cup cranberry mixture, and let stand at room temperature 30 minutes. Sprinkle with salt and pepper.

3. Grill, covered with grill lid, 10 to 12 minutes on each side or until a meat thermometer inserted in thickest portion registers 165°, basting occasionally with ¼ cup cranberry mixture. Remove from heat, and let stand 15 minutes before slicing. Serve with reserved cranberry mixture.

variation

Bourbon-Cranberry Roasted Turkey: Substitute 1 (14-lb.) whole fresh turkey for tenderloins. Remove giblets and neck; reserve for another use. Rinse turkey with cold water. Drain cavity well; pat dry with paper towels. Let turkey stand at room temperature 30 minutes. Meanwhile, prepare cranberry mixture as directed in Step 1. Place turkey, breast side up, on a lightly greased wire rack in a roasting pan. If desired, tie ends of legs together with kitchen string; tuck wing tips under. Brush with 2 Tbsp. melted butter, and sprinkle with salt and pepper. Bake at 325° for 3½ hours or until a meat thermometer inserted in thickest portion of thigh registers 170°, brushing with ½ cup cranberry mixture during the last 30 minutes of roasting. (If turkey starts to brown too much, cover loosely with aluminum foil.) Let turkey stand 15 minutes before carving. Serve with reserved cranberry mixture.

Maryland Crab Cakes with Creamy Caper-Dill Sauce

makes 14 cakes ☆ prep: 30 min. ☆ cook: 24 min. ☆ chill: 1 hr.

These golden cakes have a higher ratio of crabmeat to filling than other recipes, yet they still hold up nicely in the skillet. Plan one cake per person for an appetizer, or two cakes per person for an entrée serving.

2	lb. fresh **lump crabmeat***
½	cup minced **green onion**
½	cup minced **red bell pepper**
1	Tbsp. **olive oil**
½	cup **Italian-seasoned breadcrumbs**
1	large **egg**, lightly beaten
½	cup **mayonnaise**
1	Tbsp. fresh **lemon juice**
1½	tsp. **Old Bay seasoning**
½	tsp. **pepper**
	Dash of **Worcestershire sauce**
2	Tbsp. **butter**
	Lemon wedges
	Creamy Caper-Dill Sauce
	Garnish: **fresh dill sprigs** (optional)

1. Rinse, drain, and flake crabmeat, being careful not to break up lumps, and remove any bits of shell. Set crabmeat aside.

2. Sauté green onion and bell pepper in hot olive oil in a large nonstick skillet 8 minutes or until tender.

3. Stir together green onion mixture, breadcrumbs, egg, and next 5 ingredients. Gently fold in crabmeat. Shape mixture into 14 (2½-inch) cakes (about ⅓ cup for each cake). Place on an aluminum foil-lined baking sheet; cover and chill at least 1 hour or up to 8 hours.

4. Melt butter in a large nonstick skillet over medium heat. Add crab cakes, and cook, in 2 batches, 4 to 5 minutes on each side or until golden. Drain on paper towels. Serve with a squeeze of lemon and Creamy Caper-Dill Sauce. Garnish, if desired.

* Regular crabmeat may be substituted for lump.

Creamy Caper-Dill Sauce

makes 1¼ cups ☆ prep: 10 min.

¾ cup **mayonnaise**
½ cup **sour cream**
¼ tsp. **lemon zest**
2 Tbsp. fresh **lemon juice**
1 Tbsp. drained **capers**

2 tsp. chopped **fresh dill**
1 tsp. **Dijon mustard**
¼ tsp. **salt**
¼ tsp. **pepper**

1. Stir together all ingredients. Cover and chill up to 3 days.

New Potato Salad with Feta Cheese

makes 6 servings ☆ prep: 10 min. ☆ cook: 25 min. ☆ chill: 2 hr.

Try this lighter version of the classic picnic dish at your next get-together. At six servings, this salad is an ample main dish. As a side dish, it will serve 8 to 10.

3	lb. small **new potatoes**
⅔	cup **olive oil**
½	cup **fresh lemon juice**
1	tsp. **Dijon mustard**
1	tsp. **salt**
¾	tsp. **pepper**

1	bunch **green onions,** sliced
1	(4-oz.) package crumbled **garlic-and-herb feta cheese**
¼	cup chopped **fresh parsley**
	Mixed salad greens (optional)

1. Bring potatoes and water to cover to a boil, and cook 25 minutes or just until tender; drain well. Cool slightly, and cut into wedges.

2. Whisk together oil and next 4 ingredients in a large bowl; add potatoes, green onions, and feta cheese, tossing to coat. Cover and chill at least 2 hours or up to 8 hours. Sprinkle with parsley before serving. Serve over mixed salad greens, if desired.

Classic Sweet Potato Casserole

makes 6 to 8 servings ☆ prep: 20 min. ☆ cook: 1 hr., 40 min. ☆ stand: 40 min.

4½ lb. **sweet potatoes**
1 cup **granulated sugar**
½ cup **butter,** softened
¼ cup **milk**
2 large **eggs**
1 tsp. **vanilla extract**
¼ tsp. **salt**

1¼ cups **cornflakes cereal,** crushed
¼ cup chopped **pecans**
1 Tbsp. **brown sugar**
1 Tbsp. **butter,** melted
1½ cups **miniature marshmallows**

This mouthwatering casserole will satisfy lovers of crunchy pecans and cornflakes as well as marshmallows.

1. Preheat oven to 400°. Bake sweet potatoes at 400° for 1 hour or until tender. Let stand until cool to touch (about 20 minutes); peel and mash sweet potatoes. Reduce oven temperature to 350°.

2. Beat mashed sweet potatoes, granulated sugar, and next 5 ingredients at medium speed with an electric mixer until smooth. Spoon potato mixture into a greased 11- x 7-inch baking dish.

3. Combine cornflakes cereal and next 3 ingredients in a small bowl. Sprinkle over casserole in diagonal rows 2 inches apart.

4. Bake at 350° for 30 minutes. Remove from oven; let stand 10 minutes. Sprinkle marshmallows in alternate rows between cornflake mixture; bake 10 minutes. Let stand 10 minutes before serving.

Two-Cheese Squash Casserole

makes 10 to 12 servings ☆ prep: 25 min. ☆ cook: 43 min.

4   lb. **yellow squash,** sliced
1   large **sweet onion,** finely chopped
1   cup (4 oz.) shredded **Cheddar cheese**
½   cup chopped **fresh chives**
1   (8-oz.) container **sour cream**
1   tsp. **garlic salt**
1   tsp. freshly ground **pepper**
2   large **eggs,** lightly beaten
2½   cups soft, fresh **breadcrumbs,** divided
1¼   cups (5 oz.) freshly shredded **Parmesan cheese,** divided
2   Tbsp. **butter,** melted

Squash casserole is the most versatile side dish. It pairs with everything from fried chicken in the summertime to turkey at Thanksgiving. For a flavorful, colorful twist, substitute sliced zucchini for half of the yellow squash.

1. Preheat oven to 350°. Cook yellow squash and onion in boiling water to cover in a Dutch oven 8 minutes or just until tender; drain squash mixture well.

2. Combine squash mixture, Cheddar cheese, next 5 ingredients, 1 cup breadcrumbs, and ¾ cup Parmesan cheese. Spoon into a lightly greased 13- x 9-inch baking dish.

3. Stir together melted butter and remaining 1½ cups breadcrumbs and ½ cup Parmesan cheese. Sprinkle breadcrumb mixture over top of casserole.

4. Bake at 350° for 35 to 40 minutes or until set.

Sage Cornbread Dressing

makes 8 to 10 servings ☆ prep: 35 min. ☆ cool: 30 min. ☆ cook: 55 min.

Use all three cups of broth if you like a really moist dressing. To make ahead, prepare recipe as directed through Step 2. Cover with plastic wrap; cover with heavy-duty aluminum foil or container lid. Freeze unbaked dressing up to three months, if desired. Thaw in refrigerator 24 hours. Let stand at room temperature 30 minutes. Bake, uncovered, at 350° for 1 hour and 10 minutes to 1 hour and 15 minutes or until golden.

2   (6-oz.) packages **buttermilk cornbread mix**
⅓   cup **butter**
1   cup chopped **celery**
½   cup chopped **onion**
1   Tbsp. chopped **fresh** or 1½ tsp. **dried sage**
½   tsp. **pepper**
¼   tsp. **salt**
4   **white bread slices,** cut into ½-inch cubes (about 2 cups)
2½ to 3 cups **chicken broth**
2   large **eggs,** lightly beaten

1. Prepare cornbread according to package directions for a double recipe. Let cool 30 minutes; crumble into a large bowl.

2. Melt ⅓ cup butter in a large skillet over medium heat; add chopped celery and onion, and sauté 10 to 12 minutes or until tender. Stir in sage, pepper, and salt. Stir celery mixture and bread cubes into crumbled cornbread in bowl, stirring gently until blended. Add chicken broth and eggs, and stir gently until moistened. Spoon mixture into a lightly greased 11- x 7-inch baking dish.

3. Preheat oven to 350°. Bake at 350° for 45 to 50 minutes or until golden brown.

Note: We tested with Martha White Cotton Country Cornbread mix.

variation

Sausage Dressing: Prepare recipe as directed through Step 1. Omit ⅓ cup butter. Cook 1 (16-oz.) package pork sausage in a large skillet over medium-high heat, stirring often, 10 to 12 minutes or until meat crumbles and is no longer pink. Remove cooked sausage from skillet using a slotted spoon, and drain, reserving 2 tsp. drippings in skillet. Add chopped celery and onion, and sauté 10 to 12 minutes or until vegetables are tender; stir in sage, pepper, and salt. Stir in cooked sausage. Proceed with recipe as directed. Follow make-ahead directions, if desired.

Oyster Dressing: Prepare recipe as directed through Step 2, gently stirring 1 (12-oz.) container fresh oysters, drained, into cornbread mixture. Proceed with recipe as directed, increasing bake time to 50 to 55 minutes or until golden. Follow make-ahead directions, if desired.

Crowder Pea Succotash

makes 8 servings ☆ prep: 20 min. ☆ cook: 8 min.

Also known as cowpeas, crowder peas make a great addition to this popular Southern side dish. Serve this easy side at a family barbecue or picnic on a warm summer day.

½ large **onion,** finely diced
1 **green bell pepper,** finely diced
1 **red bell pepper,** finely diced
3 Tbsp. **olive oil**
2 cups **fresh** or **frozen corn kernels**
Crowder Peas, cooked, drained, and liquid reserved

½ cup sliced **green onions**
1 Tbsp. **fresh thyme leaves,** finely chopped
½ tsp. **salt**
Garnish: **fresh thyme sprig**

1. Sauté onion and bell peppers in hot oil in a large skillet over medium heat 5 to 7 minutes or until tender. Stir in corn and drained crowder peas; cook 2 minutes or until thoroughly heated. Stir in ½ cup reserved crowder peas liquid, green onions, thyme, and salt; cook 1 to 2 minutes or until thoroughly heated. Garnish, if desired. Serve immediately.

Crowder Peas

makes 4 servings ☆ prep: 15 min. ☆ cook: 25 min. ☆ cool: 30 min.

½ large **onion,** cut in half
½ medium **carrot,** cut in half lengthwise
2 **celery ribs,** cut into 2-inch pieces
2 **garlic cloves,** peeled and cut in half

1 Tbsp. **olive oil**
2 Tbsp. jarred **ham base**
2 cups fresh or frozen **crowder peas**
2 fresh **thyme sprigs**
½ tsp. **salt**
½ tsp. **pepper**

1. Cook first 4 ingredients in hot oil in a Dutch oven over medium-high heat for 5 minutes, stirring often. Stir in ham base and 4 cups of water until well blended. Add peas, thyme, salt, and pepper, and bring mixture to a boil. Reduce heat to low, and simmer 20 minutes or until peas are done. Remove from heat; cool 30 minutes.

2. Drain peas, reserving cooking liquid for another use. Remove and discard onion, carrots, celery, and thyme sprigs.

Note: We used Superior Touch Better Than Bouillon ham base.

Butterbeans and Bacon

makes 6 servings ☆ prep: 20 min. ☆ cook: 1 hr., 22 min.

3	thick-cut bacon slices, chopped
1	cup diced onion (1 medium onion)
3	garlic cloves, minced
1	bay leaf
¾	cup chopped green bell pepper
2	plum tomatoes, seeded and chopped (optional)
1	(32-oz.) container chicken broth
4	cups fresh or thawed frozen butterbeans
½	tsp. salt
1	tsp. pepper
1	tsp. Worcestershire sauce
½	tsp. hot sauce

Cooked beans freeze beautifully, so you can make a double batch to enjoy later.

1. Cook bacon in a skillet over medium heat, stirring often, 8 minutes or until crisp. Remove bacon, and drain on paper towels, reserving drippings in skillet. Add onion, garlic, and bay leaf; cook, stirring often, 3 minutes or until onion is tender.

2. Add bell pepper; cook, stirring often, 3 minutes. Add tomatoes, if desired; cook, stirring often, 3 minutes.

3. Add chicken broth and butterbeans; bring to a boil. Cover, reduce heat, and simmer, stirring occasionally, 30 minutes.

4. Uncover and simmer 30 minutes, stirring often. Stir in salt and next 3 ingredients. Cook, stirring often, 5 minutes. Remove and discard bay leaf. Sprinkle with cooked bacon.

Creamed Collards

makes 8 to 10 servings ☆ prep: 20 min. ☆ cook: 38 min.

4½ lb. **fresh collard greens***
1   lb. **bacon,** chopped
¼   cup **butter**
2   large **onions,** diced
3   cups **chicken broth**

½   cup **apple cider vinegar**
1   tsp. **salt**
½   tsp. **pepper**
Béchamel Sauce

1. Rinse collard greens. Trim and discard thick stems from bottom of collard green leaves (about 2 inches); coarsely chop collards.

2. Cook bacon, in batches, in an 8-qt. stockpot over medium heat 10 to 12 minutes or until crisp. Remove bacon with a slotted spoon, and drain on paper towels, reserving drippings in stockpot. Reserve ¼ cup bacon.

3. Add butter and onions to hot drippings in skillet. Sauté onions 8 minutes or until tender. Add collards, in batches, and cook, stirring occasionally, 5 minutes or until wilted. Stir in chicken broth, next 3 ingredients, and remaining bacon.

4. Bring to a boil. Reduce heat to low, and cook, stirring occasionally, 15 minutes or to desired degree of tenderness. Drain collards, reserving 1 cup liquid.

5. Stir in Béchamel Sauce. Stir in reserved cooking liquid, ¼ cup at a time, to desired consistency. Transfer to a serving dish, and sprinkle with reserved ¼ cup bacon.

* 2 (1-lb.) packages fresh collard greens, washed, trimmed, and chopped, may be substituted.

Béchamel Sauce

makes about 4½ cups ☆ prep: 10 min. ☆ cook: 7 min.

½ cup **butter**

2 medium **shallots, minced**

2 **garlic cloves,** pressed

¾ cup **all-purpose flour**

4 cups **milk**

½ tsp. **salt**

½ tsp. **pepper**

¼ tsp. ground **nutmeg**

Béchamel (bay-shah-MEHL) is the French term for white sauce.

1. Melt butter in a heavy saucepan over low heat; add shallots and garlic, and sauté 1 minute. Whisk in flour until smooth. Cook 1 minute, whisking constantly.

2. Increase heat to medium. Gradually whisk in milk; cook over medium heat, whisking constantly, 5 to 7 minutes or until mixture is thickened and bubbly. Stir in salt, pepper, and nutmeg.

make ahead

Sauce can be made ahead and stored in an airtight container in the refrigerator up to 2 days. Warm sauce over low heat before using.

Sour Cream Cornbread, page 124

Chapter 4

BREADS, BREAKFAST & BRUNCH

Sour Cream Cornbread

makes 8 servings ☆ prep: 10 min. ☆ cook: 22 min. ☆ pictured on page 122

These two classic breads are perfect for breakfast or as a dinner accompaniment.

1½ cups **self-rising white cornmeal mix**

½ cup **all-purpose flour**

1 (14.75-oz.) can **low-sodium cream-style corn**

1 (8-oz.) container **light sour cream**

3 large **eggs,** lightly beaten

2 Tbsp. chopped **fresh cilantro**

½ cup (2 oz.) 2% reduced-fat shredded **Cheddar cheese** (optional)

1. Preheat oven to 450°. Heat a 10-inch cast-iron skillet in oven 5 minutes.

2. Stir together cornmeal mix and flour in a large bowl; add corn and next 3 ingredients, stirring just until blended. Pour batter into hot lightly greased skillet. Top with cheese, if desired.

3. Bake at 450° for 22 to 24 minutes or until golden brown and cornbread pulls away from sides of skillet.

Easy Homemade Biscuits

makes about 1½ dozen ☆ prep: 10 min. ☆ cook: 9 min.

⅓ cup **butter,** softened and cubed*

2¼ cups **self-rising flour**

1 cup **buttermilk**

3 Tbsp. **melted butter**

1. Preheat oven to 450°.

2. Cut softened butter into flour with a pastry blender or 2 forks just until butter cubes are coated with flour. Using your hands, gently combine until mixture resembles small peas. Stir in buttermilk with a fork just until blended. (Mixture will be wet.)

3. Turn dough out onto a generously floured surface, and pat to ½-inch thickness. Cut dough with a well-floured 2-inch round cutter, and place on lightly greased baking sheets.

4. Bake at 450° for 9 to 11 minutes or until lightly browned. Remove from oven, and brush warm biscuits with melted butter. Serve immediately.

* ⅓ cup shortening may be substituted.

Note: We tested with White Lily Self-Rising Flour.

Easy Homemade Biscuits

Pimiento Cheese Biscuits

makes 2½ dozen ☆ prep: 20 min. ☆ chill: 10 min. ☆ cook: 13 min.

1 cup (4 oz.) shredded **sharp Cheddar cheese**
2¼ cups **self-rising soft-wheat flour**
½ cup cold **butter**, cut into ¼-inch-thick slices
1 cup **buttermilk**
1 (4-oz.) jar diced **pimiento**, drained
   Self-rising soft-wheat flour
2 Tbsp. **melted butter**

Any Southerner would be proud to have a bowl of these piping hot cheese biscuits on the breakfast table.

1. Combine shredded cheese and 2¼ cups flour in a large bowl.

2. Sprinkle butter slices over flour-cheese mixture; toss gently. Cut butter into flour with a pastry blender until crumbly. Cover and chill 10 minutes.

3. Combine buttermilk and diced pimiento; add buttermilk mixture to flour mixture, stirring just until dry ingredients are moistened.

4. Turn dough out onto a lightly floured surface, and knead 3 or 4 times, gradually adding additional flour as needed. With floured hands, press or pat dough into a ¾-inch-thick rectangle (about 9 x 5 inches). Sprinkle top of dough with additional flour. Fold dough over onto itself in 3 sections, starting with 1 short end. (Fold dough rectangle as if folding a letter-size piece of paper.) Repeat procedure 2 more times, beginning with pressing into a ¾-inch-thick dough rectangle (about 9 x 5 inches).

5. Preheat oven to 450°. Press or pat dough to ½-inch thickness on a lightly floured surface; cut with a 2-inch round cutter, and place, side by side, on a parchment paper-lined or lightly greased jelly-roll pan. (Dough rounds should touch.)

6. Bake at 450° for 13 to 15 minutes or until lightly browned. Remove from oven, and brush with 2 Tbsp. melted butter.

Hearty Oat and Walnut Bread

makes 1 loaf ☆ prep: 30 min. ☆ cook: 40 min. ☆ other: 1 hr., 55 min.

1¼ cups **water**	¾ cup chopped **walnuts**
¼ cup firmly packed **light brown sugar**	½ cup **quick-cooking oats**
1 Tbsp. **butter**	1½ tsp. **active dry yeast**
3 cups **bread flour,** divided	1½ tsp. **salt**

1. Combine water, sugar, and butter in a small saucepan; bring to a boil. Remove from heat, and let stand until mixture reaches a temperature between 120° and 130°.

2. Meanwhile, combine 2½ cups flour, walnuts, oats, yeast, and salt in a large mixing bowl; add water mixture, and stir until well blended. Turn dough out onto a heavily floured surface, and knead in enough of remaining flour to make a soft dough. Knead until smooth and elastic (about 10 minutes). Place in a well-greased bowl, turning to grease top.

3. Cover dough with plastic wrap, and let rise in a warm place (85°), free from drafts, 45 minutes or until doubled in bulk.

4. Punch dough down. Turn dough out onto a floured surface, and knead lightly 4 or 5 times. Roll dough into a 14- x 7-inch rectangle. Roll up dough, starting at narrow end, pressing firmly to eliminate air pockets; pinch ends to seal. Place dough, seam side down, in a well-greased 8- x 4-inch loaf pan. Cover and let rise in a warm place, free from drafts, 1 hour or until doubled in bulk.

5. Preheat oven to 375°.

6. Bake at 375° for 40 minutes or until loaf sounds hollow when tapped. Remove bread from pan immediately; cool on a wire rack.

Note: This bread bakes beautifully in a bread machine. To do so, combine all ingredients in the bread machine according to the manufacturer's instructions. Select bake cycle, and start machine. When done, remove bread from pan; cool on a wire rack.

There was a time when bread loaves were baked at home every day. Thanks to bread machines that knead the dough and allow it to rise without requiring attention (see directions at left), homemade yeast bread now fits into the lifestyle of hurried cooks.

Oats, walnuts, and brown sugar make this loaf a perfect partner with golden apricot or orange marmalade.

Easy Three-Seed Pan Rolls

makes 9 rolls ☆ prep: 10 min. ☆ rise: 3 hr. ☆ cook: 15 min.

The initial cost for these rolls is money well spent. You can make three scrumptious batches from the ingredients.

4	tsp. **fennel seeds**	9	**frozen bread dough rolls**
4	tsp. **poppy seeds**	1	**egg white,** beaten
4	tsp. **sesame seeds**	**Melted butter**	

1. Combine first 3 ingredients in a small bowl. Dip dough rolls, 1 at a time, in egg white; roll in seed mixture. Arrange rolls, about 1 inch apart, in a lightly greased 8-inch pan. Cover with lightly greased plastic wrap, and let rise in a warm place (85°), free from drafts, 3 to 4 hours or until doubled in bulk.

2. Preheat oven to 350°.

3. Uncover rolls, and bake at 350° for 15 minutes or until golden. Brush with melted butter.

Note: We tested with Rhodes White Dinner Rolls for frozen rolls.

variation

Three-Seed French Bread: Substitute 1 (11-oz.) can refrigerated French bread dough for frozen bread dough rolls. Combine seeds in a shallow dish. Brush dough loaf with egg white. Roll top and sides of dough loaf in seeds. Place, seam side down, on a baking sheet. Bake and cut dough loaf according to package directions.

Peach-Oat Muffins

makes 24 muffins ☆ prep: 15 min. ☆ cook: 20 min.

¼ cup chopped **pecans**
1¾ cups **uncooked regular oats**
1 cup **sugar**
½ cup **canola oil**
2 large **eggs**
1¼ cups **all-purpose flour**

1 tsp. **baking soda**
½ tsp. **salt**
1 cup **peach nectar**
1 cup **nonfat buttermilk**
5 cups **wheat bran cereal**
⅓ cup chopped **dried peaches**

These muffins are loaded with many of the components of a well-rounded breakfast: fiber and whole grains from oats and bran cereal, good fats from pecans and canola oil, dairy from nonfat buttermilk, and fruit from dried peaches.

1. Preheat oven to 375°.

2. Heat pecans in a small nonstick skillet over medium-low heat, stirring often, 2 to 4 minutes or until toasted.

3. Process oats in a food processor or blender, about 45 seconds or until finely ground.

4. Beat sugar and oil at medium speed with an electric mixer 1 minute. Add eggs, 1 at a time, beating until blended after each addition. (Mixture will be light yellow.)

5. Combine ground oats, flour, baking soda, and salt in a small bowl. Stir together peach nectar and buttermilk in a small bowl. Add oat mixture to sugar mixture alternately with peach mixture, beginning and ending with oat mixture. Stir until blended after each addition. Gently stir in bran flakes, dried peaches, and toasted pecans. Spoon batter evenly into lightly greased muffin cups, filling three-fourths full.

6. Bake at 375° for 20 minutes or until golden brown.

Note: We tested with Post Premium Bran Flakes cereal.

make ahead

Muffins may be frozen for up to 1 month. Heat in toaster oven or microwave at HIGH 30 seconds.

Poppy Seed–Lemon Muffins

makes 2 dozen ☆ prep: 10 min. ☆ cook: 18 min.

These are good on-the-go muffins because they don't have a glaze. Rest assured, they're still plenty sweet.

1	(18.25-oz.) package **yellow cake mix with pudding**	4	large **eggs**
⅔	cup **vegetable oil**	⅓	cup **poppy seeds**
⅔	cup **apricot nectar**	½	tsp. **lemon zest**
		2½	Tbsp. **fresh lemon juice**

1. Preheat oven to 400°. Combine all ingredients, stirring until blended. Spoon into greased or paper-lined muffin pans, filling two-thirds full.

2. Bake at 400° for 18 to 20 minutes or until golden brown. Remove from pans immediately, and cool on wire racks.

Note: We tested with Betty Crocker Yellow Cake Mix with Pudding.

make ahead

Make these muffins over the weekend, and place them in individual zip-top plastic bags for a delicious grab-and-go breakfast.

Cream Cheese–Banana-Nut Bread

makes 2 loaves ☆ prep: 15 min. ☆ cook: 1 hr. ☆ cool: 40 min.

Speedy to mix, this batter bakes in loaves or muffin cups. Add any one of the toppings, and you'll go faint with pleasure after the first divine bite. Warm bread is yummy, but to get perfect slices, let the bread cool 30 minutes, and cut it with a serrated or electric knife.

¾ cup **butter,** softened
1 (8-oz.) package **cream cheese,** softened
2 cups **sugar**
2 large **eggs**
3 cups **all-purpose flour**
½ tsp. **baking powder**
½ tsp. **baking soda**
½ tsp. **salt**
1½ cups mashed **bananas** (1¼ lb. unpeeled bananas, about 4 medium)
1 cup chopped **pecans,** toasted
½ tsp. **vanilla extract**

1. Preheat oven to 350°. Beat butter and cream cheese at medium speed with an electric mixer until creamy. Gradually add sugar, beating until light and fluffy. Add eggs, 1 at a time, beating just until blended after each addition.

2. Combine flour and next 3 ingredients; gradually add to butter mixture, beating at low speed just until blended. Stir in bananas, pecans, and vanilla. Spoon batter into 2 greased and floured 8- x 4-inch loaf pans.

3. Bake at 350° for 1 hour or until a long wooden pick inserted in center comes out clean and sides pull away from pan, shielding with aluminum foil during last 15 minutes to prevent browning, if necessary. Cool bread in pans on wire racks 10 minutes. Remove from pans, and cool 30 minutes on wire racks before slicing.

variations

Cream Cheese–Banana-Nut Muffins: To bake muffins, spoon batter evenly into 24 paper-lined muffin cups. Bake at 350° for 25 minutes or until a wooden pick inserted in center comes out clean. Cool in pans 10 minutes. Remove from pans, and cool completely on wire racks.

Peanut Butter Streusel–Topped Cream Cheese–Banana-Nut Bread: Prepare bread batter as directed, and spoon into desired pans. Combine ½ cup plus 1 Tbsp. all-purpose flour and ½ cup firmly packed brown sugar in a small bowl. Cut in ¼ cup butter and 3 Tbsp. creamy peanut butter with a pastry blender or fork until mixture resembles small peas. Sprinkle mixture evenly over batter in pans. Bake and cool as directed.

Cinnamon-Pecan Rolls

makes 12 rolls ☆ prep: 20 min. ☆ cook: 20 min. ☆ other: 40 min.

1 cup chopped **pecans**	2 tsp. ground **cinnamon**
1 (16-oz.) package **hot roll mix**	1 cup **powdered sugar**
½ cup **butter,** softened	2 Tbsp. **milk**
1 cup firmly packed **light brown sugar**	1 tsp. **vanilla extract**

Simple enough for a beginning baker, this easy yeast-roll dough rises in just 30 minutes.

1. Preheat oven to 350°. Bake pecans in a single layer in a shallow pan 5 to 7 minutes or until toasted and fragrant, stirring halfway through.

2. Prepare hot roll dough according to package directions; let dough stand 5 minutes. Roll dough into a 15- x 10-inch rectangle; spread with softened butter. Stir together brown sugar and cinnamon; sprinkle over butter. Sprinkle pecans over brown sugar mixture. Roll up tightly, starting at one long end; cut into 12 slices. Place rolls, cut sides down, in a lightly greased 12-inch cast-iron skillet or 13- x 9-inch pan. Cover loosely with plastic wrap and a cloth towel; let rise in a warm place (85°), free from drafts, 30 minutes or until doubled in bulk.

3. Preheat oven to 375°. Uncover rolls, and bake for 20 to 25 minutes or until center rolls are golden brown and done. Let cool in pan on a wire rack 10 minutes. Stir together powdered sugar, milk, and vanilla; drizzle over rolls.

Note: We tested with Pillsbury Specialty Mix Hot Roll Mix.

Blueberry 'n' Cheese Coffee Cake

makes 16 servings ☆ prep: 11 min. ☆ cook: 55 min.

The American tradition of serving coffee and sweet cake along with gossip actually evolved from the tradition of English tea. This moist blueberry cream cheese cake with a lemon-sugar topping is special enough for company.

½   cup **butter**, softened
1¼   cups **sugar**
2   large **eggs**
2½   cups **all-purpose flour**, divided
1   tsp. **baking powder**
1   tsp. **salt**
¾   cup **milk**

¼   cup **water**
2   cups fresh **blueberries**
1   (8-oz.) package **cream cheese**, cut into ¼-inch cubes
½   cup **sugar**
2   Tbsp. **lemon zest**
2   Tbsp. **butter**, softened

1. Preheat oven to 375°.

2. Beat ½ cup butter at medium speed with an electric mixer until creamy; gradually add 1¼ cups sugar, beating well. Add eggs, 1 at a time, beating until blended after each addition.

3. Combine 2 cups flour, baking powder, and salt; stir well. Combine milk and water; stir well. Add flour mixture to butter mixture alternately with milk mixture, beginning and ending with flour mixture. Mix at low speed after each addition until mixture is blended. Gently stir in blueberries and cream cheese. Pour batter into a greased 9-inch square pan.

4. Combine ½ cup flour and remaining 3 ingredients; stir well with a fork. Sprinkle mixture over batter. Bake at 375° for 55 minutes or until golden. Serve warm, or let cool completely on a wire rack.

Note: If you find it difficult to cut the cream cheese into such small cubes, place it in the freezer for about 20 minutes. But don't freeze it longer because partially frozen cream cheese will crumble.

Brown Sugar–Pecan Coffee Cake

makes 12 servings ☆ prep: 20 min. ☆ cook: 25 min. ☆ cool: 30 min.

2	cups **all-purpose flour**		1	large **egg,** lightly beaten
2	cups firmly packed **light brown sugar**		1	tsp. **baking soda**
¾	cup **butter,** cubed		3	Tbsp. **granulated sugar**
1	cup **sour cream**		1	tsp. **ground cinnamon**
			1	cup chopped **pecans**

This sweet coffee cake can serve as a breakfast dish or as a dessert.

1. Preheat oven to 350°. Stir together flour and brown sugar in a large bowl. Cut ¾ cup butter into flour mixture with a pastry blender or 2 forks until crumbly. Press 2¾ cups crumb mixture evenly on the bottom of a lightly greased 13- x 9-inch pan.

2. Stir together sour cream, egg, and baking soda; add to remaining crumb mixture, stirring just until dry ingredients are moistened. Stir together granulated sugar and cinnamon. Pour sour cream mixture over crumb crust in pan; sprinkle evenly with cinnamon mixture and pecans.

3. Bake at 350° for 25 to 30 minutes or until a wooden pick inserted in center comes out clean. Let cool in pan on a wire rack 30 minutes. Serve warm.

Pam-Cakes with Buttered Honey Syrup

makes about 16 (4-inch) pancakes ☆ prep: 10 min. ☆ cook: 24 min.

Use a light hand when stirring the batter; overmixing will cause a rubbery texture. When using a griddle to cook pancakes, set the temperature dial to 350°.

1¾ cups **all-purpose flour**
2 tsp. **sugar**
1½ tsp. **baking powder**
1 tsp. **baking soda**
1 tsp. **salt**
2 cups **buttermilk**

2 large **eggs**
¼ cup **butter,** melted
Buttered Honey Syrup
Apricot-Ginger Topping
Garnish: **fresh blueberries**

1. Combine flour and next 4 ingredients in a large bowl. Whisk together buttermilk and eggs. Gradually stir buttermilk mixture into flour mixture. Gently stir in butter. (Batter will be lumpy.)

2. Pour about ¼ cup batter for each pancake onto a hot buttered griddle or large nonstick skillet. Cook pancakes 3 to 4 minutes or until tops are covered with bubbles and edges look dry and cooked. Turn and cook 3 to 4 minutes or until golden brown. Place pancakes in a single layer on a baking sheet, and keep warm in a 200° oven up to 30 minutes. Serve with Buttered Honey Syrup and Apricot-Ginger Topping. Garnish, if desired.

Buttered Honey Syrup

makes about ¾ cup ☆ prep: 5 min. ☆ cook: 1 min.

⅓ cup **butter**

½ cup **honey**

1. Melt butter in a small saucepan over medium-low heat. Stir in honey, and cook 1 minute or until warm.

Note: Buttered Honey Syrup cannot be made ahead. The heated honey will crystallize when cooled and will not melt if reheated.

Apricot-Ginger Topping

makes about ½ cup ☆ prep: 5 min. ☆ cook: 1 min.

½ cup **apricot** or **peach**
preserves

1½ tsp. finely chopped
crystallized ginger*

Once you drizzle Pam-Cakes with Buttered Honey Syrup, add more flavor with a delicious topping.

1. Microwave preserves and ginger at HIGH 1 minute and 20 seconds, stirring at 20-second intervals.

* ¼ tsp. ground ginger may be substituted.

Note: Crystallized ginger adds texture and a subtle ginger flavor. Using ground ginger yields a thinner mixture but a spicier flavor.

Praline-Pecan French Toast

makes 8 to 10 servings ☆ prep: 20 min. ☆ chill: 8 hr. ☆ cook: 35 min.

1   (16-oz.) **French bread loaf**
1   cup firmly packed **light brown sugar**
⅓   cup **butter,** melted
2   Tbsp. **maple syrup**
¾   cup chopped **pecans**

4   large **eggs,** lightly beaten
1   cup 2% **reduced-fat milk**
2   Tbsp. **granulated sugar**
1   tsp. ground **cinnamon**
1   tsp. **vanilla extract**

Assemble the casserole the night before, chill overnight, and pop it in the oven in the morning to have breakfast ready in a snap.

1. Cut 10 (1-inch-thick) slices of bread. Reserve remaining bread for another use.

2. Stir together brown sugar and next 2 ingredients; pour into a lightly greased 13- x 9-inch baking dish. Sprinkle with chopped pecans.

3. Whisk together eggs and remaining 4 ingredients. Arrange bread slices over pecans; pour egg mixture over bread. Cover and chill 8 hours.

4. Preheat oven to 350°. Bake bread 35 to 37 minutes or until golden brown. Serve immediately.

Sausage-and-Egg Casserole

makes 10 servings ☆ prep: 20 min. ☆ cook: 1 hr.

Use 1 (16-oz.) package of crumbled pork sausage instead of the patties, if desired. Simply cook in a nonstick skillet until browned.

8 (1½-oz.) **sourdough bread slices,** cut into ½-inch cubes
1 (12-oz.) package fully cooked **pork sausage patties,** chopped
2½ cups 2% **reduced-fat milk**
4 large **eggs**

1 Tbsp. **Dijon mustard**
½ cup **buttermilk**
1 (10¾-oz.) can **cream of mushroom soup**
1 cup (4 oz.) shredded **sharp Cheddar cheese**

1. Preheat oven to 350°. Arrange bread in 2 lightly greased 8-inch square baking dishes or 1 lightly greased 13- x 9-inch baking dish. Top evenly with sausage. Whisk together 2½ cups milk, eggs, and Dijon mustard. Pour evenly over bread mixture.

2. Whisk together buttermilk and cream of mushroom soup. Spoon over bread mixture; sprinkle with Cheddar cheese. Place casserole on a baking sheet.

3. Bake at 350° for 1 hour or until casserole is set. Serve immediately.

Note: This casserole can also be made in 10 individual 8- to 10-oz. ovenproof coffee mugs. Omit baking dishes. Divide bread cubes evenly among mugs coated with cooking spray, placing in bottom of mugs. Proceed as directed, reducing bake time to 25 to 30 minutes or until casseroles are set.

make ahead

An unbaked casserole can be covered with plastic wrap, then foil, and frozen up to 1 month. Thaw overnight in the refrigerator. Bake as directed.

Cornbread Omelets

makes 5 servings ☆ prep: 20 min. ☆ cook: 20 min.

A featherlight cornbread batter takes the place of eggs in these fun omelets.

¾ lb. **chorizo sausage,** casings removed (about 3 links)
6 Tbsp. **butter,** divided
3 **green onions,** chopped
1 small **red bell pepper,** chopped
2 **jalapeño peppers,** minced
1 cup **self-rising white cornmeal mix**
½ cup **buttermilk**
½ cup **milk**
¼ cup **all-purpose flour**
1 large **egg,** lightly beaten
Vegetable cooking spray
1 cup (4 oz.) shredded **Mexican cheese blend**

1. Sauté chorizo in an 8-inch nonstick omelet pan or skillet with sloped sides 7 to 10 minutes or until browned. Remove from skillet, and drain on paper towels. Wipe skillet clean.

2. Melt 1 Tbsp. butter in skillet, and sauté green onions, bell pepper, and jalapeño peppers over medium-high heat 3 to 5 minutes or until tender. Transfer to a bowl; stir in chorizo. Wipe skillet clean.

3. Whisk together cornmeal mix, buttermilk, milk, flour, and egg.

4. Coat skillet with cooking spray; melt 1 Tbsp. butter in skillet over medium-high heat, rotating pan to coat bottom evenly. Pour about ⅓ cup cornmeal mixture into skillet. Tilt pan so uncooked portion flows around to coat bottom of pan, cooking until almost set, bubbles form, and edges are dry (about 1½ minutes). Gently flip with a spatula.

5. Sprinkle 1 side of omelet with about ½ cup onion mixture and about 3 Tbsp. cheese. Fold omelet in half; cook 30 seconds or until cheese is melted. Transfer to a serving plate; keep warm. Repeat procedure 4 times with remaining butter, cornmeal mixture, onion mixture, and cheese. Serve immediately.

Ham-and-Tomato Pie

makes 4 to 6 servings ☆ prep: 20 min. ☆ cook: 25 min. ☆ other: 20 min.

1   (8-oz.) package diced **cooked ham**

4   **green onions,** sliced

1   (9-inch) **frozen unbaked pie shell**

1   Tbsp. **Dijon mustard**

1   cup (4 oz.) shredded **mozzarella cheese,** divided

2   medium **plum tomatoes,** thinly sliced

1   large **egg**

⅓   cup **half-and-half**

1   Tbsp. chopped **fresh basil**

⅛   tsp. **pepper**

Garnishes: **fresh basil sprigs, tomato slices**

This quichelike pie is equally yummy for brunch or lunch. You can prepare it with packaged chopped ham or leftover ham.

1. Preheat oven to 425°. Sauté ham and green onions in a large nonstick skillet over medium heat 5 minutes or until ham is browned and any liquid evaporates.

2. Brush bottom of pie shell evenly with mustard; sprinkle with ½ cup mozzarella cheese. Spoon ham mixture evenly over cheese, and top with single layer of sliced tomatoes.

3. Beat egg and half-and-half with a fork until blended; pour over tomatoes. Sprinkle evenly with basil, pepper, and remaining ½ cup cheese.

4. Bake on lowest oven rack at 425° for 20 to 23 minutes or until lightly browned and set. Cool on a wire rack 20 minutes. Cut into wedges to serve. Garnish, if desired.

Traditional Eggs Benedict

makes 2 servings ☆ prep: 25 min. ☆ cook: 10 min.

Pair this indulgent favorite with a fresh fruit salad.

8 (½-oz.) **Canadian bacon** slices
Vegetable cooking spray
2 **English muffins,** split and toasted
4 large **eggs,** poached

Hollandaise Sauce
Coarsely ground **pepper**
Paprika
Garnish: chopped **chives**

1. Cook bacon in a skillet coated with cooking spray over medium heat until thoroughly heated, turning once. Drain on paper towels.

2. Place 2 bacon slices on each muffin half. Top each half with a poached egg, and drizzle evenly with Hollandaise Sauce. Sprinkle with pepper and paprika; garnish, if desired, and serve immediately.

Hollandaise Sauce

makes 1½ cups ☆ prep: 5 min. ☆ cook: 10 min.

4 large **egg yolks**
2 Tbsp. **fresh lemon juice**

1 cup **butter,** melted
¼ tsp. **salt**

1. Whisk yolks in top of a double boiler; gradually whisk in lemon juice. Place over hot water (do not boil). Add butter, ⅓ cup at a time, whisking until smooth; whisk in salt. Cook, whisking constantly, 10 minutes or until thickened and a thermometer registers 160°. Serve immediately.

Sunny Skillet Breakfast

makes 6 servings ☆ prep: 15 min. ☆ cook: 26 min. ☆ other: 5 min.

3 (8-oz.) **baking potatoes,** peeled and shredded (about 3 cups firmly packed)*
1 Tbsp. **butter**
2 Tbsp. **vegetable oil**
1 small **red bell pepper,** diced
1 medium **onion,** diced
1 **garlic clove,** pressed
¾ tsp. **salt,** divided
6 large **eggs**
¼ tsp. **pepper**

Soaking the shredded potatoes in cold water keeps them from turning gray before cooking. It also rinses off some of the starch. Drain and pat them dry so they won't stick to the cast-iron skillet.

1. Preheat oven to 350°. Place shredded potatoes in a large bowl; add cold water to cover. Let stand 5 minutes; drain and pat dry.

2. Melt butter with oil in a 10-inch cast-iron skillet over medium heat. Add bell pepper and onion, and sauté 3 to 5 minutes or until tender. Add garlic; sauté 1 minute. Stir in shredded potatoes and ½ tsp. salt; cook, stirring often, 10 minutes or until potatoes are golden and tender.

3. Remove from heat. Make 6 indentations in potato mixture, using back of a spoon. Break 1 egg into each indentation. Sprinkle eggs with pepper and remaining ¼ tsp. salt.

4. Bake at 350° for 12 to 14 minutes or until eggs are set. Serve immediately.

* 3 cups firmly packed frozen shredded potatoes may be substituted, omitting Step 1.

variation

Veggie Confetti Frittata: Prepare recipe as directed through Step 2, sautéing ½ (8-oz.) package sliced fresh mushrooms with bell peppers and onion. Remove from heat, and stir in ¼ cup sliced ripe black olives, drained, and ¼ cup thinly sliced sun-dried tomatoes in oil, drained. Whisk together eggs, pepper, and remaining ¼ tsp. salt; whisk in ½ cup (2 oz.) shredded Swiss cheese. Pour egg mixture over potato mixture in skillet. Bake at 350° for 9 to 10 minutes or until set. Cut into wedges, and serve immediately. Makes 6 servings. Prep: 15 min. Cook: 26 min. Other: 5 min.

Hash Brown Casserole

makes 12 servings ☆ prep: 20 min. ☆ cook: 1 hr.

¾ cup chopped **onion**

½ tsp. **paprika**

½ tsp. freshly ground **pepper**

1 (32-oz.) package **frozen Southern-style hash brown potatoes** (diced)

2 Tbsp. **butter,** melted

1 (10¾-oz.) can **cream of chicken soup**

1 (8-oz.) package **pasteurized prepared cheese product,** cubed

1 (8-oz.) container **sour cream**

2½ cups **cornflakes cereal,** coarsely crushed

2 Tbsp. **butter,** melted

This down-home side dish boasts a buttery cornflake crust on top.

1. Preheat oven to 350°. Combine first 5 ingredients in a large bowl; toss well.

2. Combine soup and cheese in a medium microwave-safe bowl. Microwave at HIGH 6 minutes or until cheese melts, stirring every 2 minutes. Stir in sour cream. Pour cheese mixture over potato mixture, and stir well. Spread into a lightly greased 13- x 9-inch baking dish.

3. Combine cornflakes and 2 Tbsp. butter; sprinkle over top of potato mixture. Bake, uncovered, at 350° for 1 hour.

Creamy Grits Casserole

makes 8 servings ☆ prep: 10 min. ☆ cook: 40 min. ☆ stand: 5 min.

This buttery, two-cheese casserole featuring one of the South's favorite foods is a must for holiday brunches or to serve at dinner with shrimp or ham.

1¼	cups **uncooked regular grits**	1	(10-oz.) block **sharp Cheddar cheese,** shredded
2	cups **chicken broth**		
2	cups **milk**	1	(4-oz.) **smoked Gouda cheese round,** shredded
1	tsp. **salt**		
¼	tsp. **ground red pepper**	2	large **eggs,** lightly beaten
½	cup **butter,** cut into cubes		

1. Preheat oven to 350°. Bring grits, chicken broth, and next 3 ingredients to a boil in a medium saucepan over medium-high heat; reduce heat to low, and simmer, stirring occasionally, 4 to 5 minutes or until thickened. Stir in butter and cheeses until melted.

2. Gradually stir about one-fourth of hot grits mixture into eggs; add egg mixture to remaining hot grits mixture, stirring constantly. Pour grits mixture into a lightly greased 2½-qt. baking dish.

3. Bake at 350° for 35 to 40 minutes or until golden brown and bubbly around edges. Let stand 5 minutes before serving.

Warm Cinnamon Apples

makes 6 servings ☆ prep: 10 min. ☆ cook: 8 min.

This simple spiced apples recipe is great for breakfast, as a warm and yummy side, or served atop pork. If you can't find McIntosh apples, substitute another baking apple such as Rome or Gala, or try a crisp, tart green apple such as Granny Smith.

4	**McIntosh apples,** peeled and sliced (about 2 lb.)	1	tsp. ground **cinnamon**
		¼	tsp. ground **nutmeg**
½	cup firmly packed **light brown sugar**	1	Tbsp. **butter**

1. Combine first 4 ingredients in a large zip-top plastic bag, tossing to coat apples.

2. Cook apple mixture, 2 Tbsp. water, and 1 Tbsp. butter in a medium saucepan over medium heat, stirring occasionally, 8 to 10 minutes or until apples are tender.

Creamy Grits Casserole

Chicken-Fried Steak, page 164

Chapter 5

MAIN DISHES

Chicken-Fried Steak

makes 6 servings ☆ prep: 10 min. ☆ cook: 38 min. ☆ pictured on page 162

Authentic chicken-fried steak is crunchy outside, tender inside, and served with plenty of cream gravy made from pan drippings. Bring it on!

2¼ tsp. **salt,** divided
¼ tsp. ground **black pepper**
6 (4-oz.) **cube steaks**
38 **saltine crackers** (1 sleeve), crushed
1¼ cups **all-purpose flour,** divided
½ tsp. **baking powder**

1½ tsp. ground **black pepper,** divided
½ tsp. **ground red pepper**
4¾ cups **milk,** divided
2 large **eggs**
3½ cups **peanut oil**

1. Sprinkle ¼ tsp. each salt and black pepper over steaks. Set aside.

2. Combine cracker crumbs, 1 cup flour, baking powder, 1 tsp. salt, ½ tsp. black pepper, and red pepper in a shallow dish.

3. Whisk together ¾ cup milk and eggs. Dredge steaks in cracker crumb mixture; dip in milk mixture, and dredge in cracker mixture again.

4. Preheat oven to 225°. Pour oil into a 12-inch skillet; heat to 360°. (Do not use a nonstick skillet.) Fry steaks, in batches, 10 minutes. Turn and fry each batch 4 to 5 more minutes or until golden brown. Remove to a wire rack on a jelly-roll pan. Keep steaks warm in a 225° oven. Carefully drain hot oil, reserving cooked bits and 1 Tbsp. drippings in skillet.

5. Whisk together remaining ¼ cup flour, 1 tsp. salt, 1 tsp. black pepper, and 4 cups milk. Pour mixture into reserved drippings in skillet; cook over medium-high heat, whisking constantly, 10 to 12 minutes or until thickened. Serve gravy with steaks and mashed potatoes, if desired.

Aunt Mary's Pot Roast

makes 6 servings ☆ prep: 10 min. ☆ cook: 3 hr.

1 (3- to 4-lb.) **chuck roast**
1 (12-oz.) can **beer**

1 (0.7-oz.) envelope **Italian dressing mix**

1. Preheat oven to 300°. Brown roast on all sides in a lightly oiled 5-qt. cast-iron Dutch oven over high heat. Remove from heat, and add beer and dressing mix.

2. Bake, covered, at 300° for 3 hours or until tender, turning once.

To reduce the fat in this recipe, substitute an eye of round roast for the chuck roast. Both cuts of meat become fall-apart tender when cooked with slow, moist heat. Long before the use of electricity, pioneers were using cast-iron Dutch ovens as "slow cookers."

Beef Tenderloin with Five-Onion Sauce

makes 8 servings ☆ prep: 15 min. ☆ cook: 1 hr., 15 min. ☆ stand: 10 min.

1	(3½-lb.) trimmed **beef tenderloin**	2	bunches **green onions,** chopped
1½	tsp. **salt,** divided	12	**shallots,** chopped
1	tsp. **pepper,** divided	5	**garlic cloves,** minced
2	Tbsp. **canola oil**	½	cup **cognac**
3	Tbsp. **butter**	½	cup **beef broth**
2	large **yellow onions,** sliced and separated into rings		Garnish: **fresh thyme sprigs**
2	large **red onions,** sliced and separated into rings		

Buy a 5- to 6-lb. tenderloin, and ask your butcher to trim it to size.

1. Preheat oven to 400°. Sprinkle tenderloin with ½ tsp. salt and ½ tsp. pepper. Secure with string at 1-inch intervals. Brown tenderloin on all sides in hot oil in a heavy roasting pan or ovenproof Dutch oven. Remove tenderloin, reserving drippings in pan.

2. Add butter to drippings, and cook over medium-high heat until melted. Add yellow and red onions, and sauté 5 minutes. Add green onions, shallots, and garlic, and sauté 10 minutes. Stir in cognac and broth; cook over high heat, stirring constantly, until liquid evaporates (about 5 minutes). Place tenderloin on top.

3. Bake, covered, at 400° for 45 minutes or until a meat thermometer inserted into thickest portion registers 145° (medium-rare). Remove tenderloin from roasting pan, reserving onion mixture in pan; cover tenderloin loosely, and let stand at room temperature 10 minutes.

4. Cook onion mixture over medium heat, stirring constantly, 3 to 5 minutes or until liquid evaporates. Stir in remaining 1 tsp. salt and remaining ½ tsp. pepper. Serve onion mixture with sliced tenderloin. Garnish, if desired.

Beef-and-Sausage Meatloaf with Chunky Red Sauce

makes 12 servings (2 meatloaves) ☆ prep: 15 min. ☆ cook: 50 min. stand: 10 min.

If serving 1 meatloaf, let remaining cooked meatloaf stand until completely cool (about 30 minutes). Wrap tightly in plastic wrap and aluminum foil, and place in a large zip-top plastic bag. Store in refrigerator 2 to 3 days, or freeze up to 1 month.

1 lb. **ground sirloin***
1 lb. **ground pork sausage**
1 sleeve **multigrain saltine crackers,** crushed
1 (15-oz.) can **tomato sauce**
1 **green bell pepper,** diced
½ cup diced **red onion**
2 large **eggs,** lightly beaten
Chunky Red Sauce

1. Preheat oven to 425°. Line bottom and sides of 2 (8- x 4-inch) loaf pans with aluminum foil, allowing 2 to 3 inches to extend over sides; fold foil down around sides of pan. Lightly grease foil.

2. Gently combine first 7 ingredients in a medium bowl. Shape mixture into 2 loaves. Place meatloaves in prepared pans.

3. Bake at 425° for 50 minutes or until a meat thermometer inserted into thickest portion registers 160°. Let stand 10 minutes. Remove meatloaves from pans, using foil sides as handles. Serve with Chunky Red Sauce.

* Ground chuck or lean ground beef may be substituted.

Chunky Red Sauce

makes about 3 cups ☆ prep: 5 min. ☆ cook: 15 min.

1 (26-oz.) jar **vegetable spaghetti sauce**
1 (14.5-oz.) can **fire-roasted diced tomatoes***
2 tsp. **dried Italian seasoning**
¼ tsp. **pepper**

1. Stir together all ingredients in a large saucepan over medium heat. Cook, stirring frequently, 15 minutes or until thoroughly heated.

* 1 (14.5-oz.) can diced tomatoes may be substituted.

Note: We tested with Ragú Garden Combination Pasta Sauce and Hunt's Fire Roasted Diced Tomatoes.

Open-face Beef-and-Sausage Meatloaf Sandwich

makes 6 servings ☆ prep: 15 min. ☆ cook: 35 min.

1   cooked **Beef-and-Sausage Meatloaf** (page 168), chilled

1   (12-oz.) **French bread loaf**

1   (8-oz.) block **mozzarella cheese,** grated and divided

Chunky Red Sauce (page 168)

2   Tbsp. chopped **fresh parsley**

1. Preheat oven to 325°. Cut chilled meatloaf into 6 (1-inch-thick) slices. Place on an aluminum foil–lined baking sheet.

2. Bake for 30 minutes. Remove to a wire rack. Increase oven temperature to 400°.

3. Cut bread diagonally into 6 (1-inch-thick) slices. Place on an aluminum foil–lined baking sheet. Sprinkle evenly with 1 cup mozzarella cheese.

4. Bake at 400° for 5 to 7 minutes or until cheese is melted and bubbly. Place 1 meatloaf slice on each piece of cheese toast. Top with desired amount of Chunky Red Sauce. Sprinkle with parsley and remaining cheese.

Osso Buco

makes 8 servings ☆ prep: 15 min. ☆ cook: 3 hr.

The Italian influence on Southern cooking can be seen in this stewlike dish. Osso buco (AW-soh-BOO-koh) yields tender meat chunks smothered in a thick vegetable-enriched broth for a one-dish meal.

3   **fresh parsley sprigs**
1   **fresh thyme sprig**
1   **bay leaf**
8   **(2-inch-thick) veal shanks**
½   tsp. **salt**
1   tsp. **pepper**
¼   cup **olive oil,** divided
2   large **onions,** chopped
3   large **carrots,** cut into ½-inch cubes
3   **celery ribs,** cut into ½-inch cubes
2   cups **dry white wine**
4   cups **hot water**
4   tsp. **beef bouillon granules**
1   Tbsp. **all-purpose flour**
1   Tbsp. **butter,** softened

1. Preheat oven to 375°. Tie together first 3 ingredients with kitchen string; set aside.

2. Rub veal with salt and pepper.

3. Brown half of veal in 1½ Tbsp. hot oil in a large skillet over medium-high heat, turning often, 5 minutes. Remove to a roasting pan; keep warm. Repeat with 1½ Tbsp. oil and remaining veal.

4. Sauté onions, carrots, and celery in remaining 1 Tbsp. hot oil in skillet until tender. Add wine; bring to a boil, and boil, stirring occasionally, until reduced by two-thirds (about 15 minutes). Add 4 cups hot water, bouillon, and herb bundle; cover and bring to a boil. Pour over veal.

5. Bake, covered, at 375° for 1 hour and 45 minutes or until veal is tender. Remove veal from pan; keep warm. Pour drippings through a wire-mesh strainer into a skillet, discarding solids. Bring to a boil, and boil until reduced by half (about 40 minutes).

6. Whisk together flour and butter until smooth; whisk into drippings. Cook, whisking constantly, 1 minute or until thickened. Serve with veal.

Grilled Lamb Chops with Lemon-Tarragon Aïoli and Orange Gremolata

makes 4 servings ☆ prep: 10 min. ☆ stand: 20 min. ☆ cook: 10 min.

At medium-rare, the meat will feel soft and slightly springy when pressed with tongs or your finger. Medium lamb will be slightly firm and springy. Lamb chops cooked beyond medium doneness may be tough and dry. Remember, the meat will continue to cook during the five-minute standing time.

8	(1½- to 2-inch-thick) **lamb loin chops** (about 2½ lb.)	½	tsp. freshly ground **pepper**
2	Tbsp. **olive oil**	1	**navel orange**
1	tsp. **salt**		**Lemon-Tarragon Aïoli**
			Orange Gremolata

1. Preheat grill to medium-high heat (350° to 400°). Trim fat from edges of lamb chops to ⅛-inch thickness. Brush both sides of lamb evenly with olive oil. Sprinkle evenly with salt and pepper. Let stand 15 minutes.

2. Grill lamb chops, covered with grill lid, 4 to 5 minutes on each side (medium-rare) or to desired degree of doneness. Transfer lamb chops to a serving platter; cover loosely with aluminum foil, and let stand 5 minutes.

3. Cut orange into 8 wedges. Grill orange wedges, covered with grill lid, 1 to 2 minutes on each side or until grill marks appear. Serve lamb chops with grilled orange wedges, Lemon-Tarragon Aïoli, and Orange Gremolata.

Lemon-Tarragon Aïoli

makes about 1 cup ☆ prep: 10 min. ☆ chill: 30 min.

1	**shallot,** chopped	2	Tbsp. **fresh lemon juice**
¾	cup **mayonnaise**	1	tsp. minced **fresh garlic**
2	Tbsp. chopped **fresh tarragon**	1½	tsp. **Dijon mustard**

1. Process all ingredients in a blender until smooth; transfer to a small bowl. Cover and chill at least 30 minutes or up to 3 days.

Orange Gremolata

makes about ½ cup ☆ prep: 10 min.

½ cup minced **fresh flat-leaf parsley**

2 tsp. **orange zest**

2 tsp. minced **fresh garlic**

⅛ tsp. **salt**

Pinch of **pepper**

1. Combine all ingredients. Serve immediately, or cover and chill up to 3 days.

Harvest Lamb Stew

makes 8 servings ☆ prep: 20 min. ☆ cook: 4 hr., 52 min.

2½ lb. lean **lamb stew meat** (about 1-inch pieces)
1½ tsp. **salt**
¼ tsp. freshly ground **pepper**
¼ cup **all-purpose flour**
4 Tbsp. **olive oil**
1 (6-oz.) can **tomato paste**
1 (14.5-oz.) can **beef broth**
1 cup chopped **celery**

1 cup chopped **sweet onion**
3 **garlic cloves**, crushed
1 small **butternut squash** (about 1 lb.), peeled, seeded, and chopped
Hot cooked mashed potatoes (optional)
Garnish: **fresh parsley sprigs**

Instead of the usual beef stew, why not try this equally comforting version using lamb and butternut squash?

1. Rinse lamb stew meat, and pat dry. Sprinkle with salt and pepper; toss in flour, shaking off excess.

2. Cook half of lamb in 2 Tbsp. hot oil in a Dutch oven over medium-high heat, stirring occasionally, 10 minutes or until browned. Repeat procedure with remaining lamb and oil. Stir in tomato paste; cook 1 minute. Add broth, and stir to loosen browned bits from bottom of Dutch oven. Transfer mixture to a 6-quart slow cooker.

3. Stir in celery, onion, and garlic. Top with butternut squash. (Do not stir to incorporate.) Cover and cook on LOW 4½ hours or until meat is tender. Serve over hot cooked mashed potatoes, if desired. Garnish, if desired.

Note: To peel and cut butternut squash, use a sharp knife to cut 1 inch from the top and bottom of the squash; discard. Using a serrated peeler, peel away the thick skin until you reach the deeper orange flesh of the squash. With a spoon or melon baller, scoop away the seeds and membranes; discard.

variation

Harvest Beef Stew: Substitute 2½ lb. beef stew meat for lamb. Proceed with recipe as directed.

Grilled Baby Back Ribs

makes 6 servings ☆ prep: 30 min. ☆ chill: 8 hr. ☆ stand: 40 min. cook: 2 hr., 30 min.

1   Tbsp. **kosher salt**
1   Tbsp. ground **black pepper**
½   tsp. **dried crushed red pepper**
3   slabs **baby back pork ribs** (about 5½ lb.)

2   **limes**, halved
Bottled barbecue sauce

Our unique stacking method gives you fall-off-the-bone-tender results every time you grill.

1. Combine kosher salt and next 2 ingredients. Remove thin membrane from back of ribs by slicing into it with a knife and pulling it off.

2. Rub ribs with cut sides of limes, squeezing as you rub. Massage salt mixture into meat, covering all sides. Wrap tightly with plastic wrap. Place in a 13- x 9-inch baking dish; cover and chill 8 hours.

3. Light 1 side of grill, heating to medium-high heat (350° to 400°); leave other side unlit. Let slabs stand at room temperature 30 minutes. Remove plastic wrap. Place slabs over unlit side of grill, stacking one on top of the other. Grill, covered with grill lid, 40 minutes. Rotate slabs, moving bottom slab to top; grill 40 minutes. Rotate again; grill 40 minutes.

4. Lower grill temperature to medium heat (300° to 350°); place slabs side by side over unlit side of grill. Baste with barbecue sauce. Grill 30 minutes, covered with grill lid, basting with sauce occasionally. Remove from grill; let stand 10 minutes.

Pork Roast with Hoppin' John Stuffing

makes 6 to 8 servings ☆ prep: 30 min. ☆ cook: 1 hr.

All the traditional New Year's favorites combine in this dish that's sure to get rave reviews any time of year.

1 small **onion,** chopped
½ medium-size **green bell pepper,** chopped
2 Tbsp. **vegetable oil**
1½ cups **cooked long-grain rice**
1½ cups frozen chopped **collard greens,** thawed
1 (15-oz.) can **black-eyed peas,** drained and rinsed
½ cup diced **cooked country ham**
½ tsp. **sugar**
½ tsp. **salt**
1 large **egg,** lightly beaten
1 (2½-lb.) **boneless pork loin roast**
Garnish: **fresh thyme sprigs**

1. Preheat oven to 375°. Sauté onion and bell pepper in hot oil in a large skillet over medium-high heat 5 to 7 minutes or until tender. Remove from heat. Add rice and next 5 ingredients; stir in egg. Set stuffing aside.

2. Butterfly pork loin roast by making a lengthwise cut down center of 1 flat side, cutting to within ½ inch of bottom. From bottom of cut, slice horizontally to ½ inch from left side; repeat procedure to right side. Open roast, and place between 2 sheets of heavy-duty plastic wrap; flatten to ½-inch thickness using a meat mallet or rolling pin.

3. Spoon 1½ cups stuffing evenly over roast, leaving a ½-inch border. Roll up; tie with string at 1-inch intervals. Place, seam side down, in a lightly greased 11- x 7-inch baking dish.

4. Bake at 375° for 55 to 60 minutes or until a meat thermometer inserted in center registers 160°. Reheat remaining Hoppin' John, and serve with roast. Garnish, if desired.

Apple-Sage-Stuffed Pork Chops

makes 6 servings ☆ prep: 30 min. ☆ cook: 48 min. ☆ stand: 25 min.

3 Tbsp. **butter**
½ cup finely chopped **yellow onion**
½ cup finely chopped **celery**
½ cup finely chopped **Granny Smith apple**
½ cup finely chopped **fresh mushrooms**
1½ cups **herb stuffing mix**
1 (14.5-oz.) can **chicken broth**
5 **fresh sage leaves**, finely chopped*

6 Tbsp. finely chopped **fresh flat-leaf parsley**, divided
1 tsp. **salt**, divided
1 tsp. ground black **pepper**, divided
¼ tsp. **ground red pepper**
6 (2-inch-thick) **bone-in center-cut pork chops**
¼ cup **olive oil**, divided
Garnishes: **steamed baby carrots, pearl onions**

Dress up traditional pork chops with the fresh flavors of Granny Smith apples and sage.

1. Melt butter in a large skillet over medium-high heat; add onion and next 3 ingredients, and sauté 10 minutes or until vegetables are tender and liquid evaporates. Remove from heat. Add stuffing mix and broth; stir until liquid is absorbed. Stir in sage, 2 Tbsp. chopped parsley, ½ tsp. salt, ½ tsp. black pepper, and ground red pepper. Let stand 20 minutes.

2. Preheat oven to 375°. Trim excess fat from each pork chop, and cut a slit in 1 side of each chop to form a pocket. Spoon stuffing mixture evenly into each pocket.

3. Combine remaining 4 Tbsp. parsley, ½ tsp. salt, and ½ tsp. black pepper. Rub both sides of stuffed pork chops evenly with 2 Tbsp. oil, and spread parsley mixture evenly over chops.

4. Cook chops in remaining 2 Tbsp. hot oil in a large nonstick skillet over medium-high heat, in batches, 2 minutes on each side or until browned. Place on a lightly greased rack in a broiler pan. Add 1 cup water to bottom of broiler pan.

5. Bake at 375° for 30 to 40 minutes. Let stand 5 minutes before serving. Garnish, if desired.

* ½ tsp. rubbed sage may be substituted.

Note: We tested with Pepperidge Farm Herb Seasoned Stuffing Mix.

Crown Pork Roast

makes 8 to 10 servings ☆ prep: 20 min. ☆ cook: 2 hr., 30 min. ☆ stand: 15 min.

This roast makes a lot, so if you have leftovers, simply cut it into chops, and freeze in zip-top plastic bags up to three months. Pull a bag out of the freezer, and thaw in the refrigerator overnight. You can then brown the chops in a skillet to warm them.

3 Tbsp. **steak seasoning**
1 (11-rib) **crown pork roast,** trimmed and tied
1 large **apple**

1 cup fresh **kumquats**
Garnishes: **fresh thyme sprigs, currants, grapes, orange wedges**

1. Preheat oven to 350°. Rub steak seasoning evenly over all sides of pork roast. Place roast in a roasting pan; position a large apple in center of roast to help hold its shape.

2. Bake pork roast at 350° for 2 hours. Top apple with kumquats, and bake 30 more minutes or until a meat thermometer inserted between ribs 2 inches into meat registers 160°. Let pork roast stand 15 minutes or until thermometer registers 165° before slicing. Garnish, if desired.

Note: We tested with McCormick Grill Mates Montreal Steak Seasoning.

Fantastic Foolproof Smokey Jambalaya

makes 4 to 6 servings ☆ prep: 15 min. ☆ cook: 1 hr., 10 min.

Shrimp, chicken, smoked sausage, and smoked pork simmer together in this quick version of Louisiana's famous meaty rice stew.

1 cup peeled, uncooked, medium-size **fresh** or **frozen raw shrimp**

1 **onion,** finely chopped

1 **green bell pepper,** finely chopped

1 **celery rib,** finely chopped

1 cup diced **smoked sausage**

1 cup cubed **boneless, skinless chicken thighs**

4 Tbsp. **vegetable oil**

1½ cups **uncooked extra-long-grain white rice**

1 cup shredded **smoked pork**

2 (10½-oz.) cans **condensed beef broth,** undiluted

3 Tbsp. **Creole seasoning**

1 **bay leaf**

Garnish: **green onion tops**

1. Preheat oven to 325°. If frozen, thaw shrimp according to package directions. Devein, if desired, and set aside.

2. Cook onion and next 4 ingredients in hot oil in a 4-qt. cast-iron Dutch oven over medium-high heat, stirring constantly, 10 minutes or until chicken is lightly browned. Stir in rice, 1 cup water, pork and next 3 ingredients. Bake, covered, at 325° for 50 minutes. (Do not remove lid or stir.)

3. Remove from oven, and stir in shrimp. Bake, covered, 10 more minutes or just until shrimp turn pink. Discard bay leaf. Garnish, if desired.

Citrus Glazed Ham

makes 12 to 14 servings ☆ prep: 10 min. ☆ cook: 2 hr., 30 min.
stand: 15 min.

1	(6- to 7-lb.) **fully cooked, bone-in ham**	½	cup firmly packed **light brown sugar**
30	to 32 **whole cloves**	¼	cup **Dijon mustard**
1	(10-oz.) bottle **orange juice–flavored soft drink**		Garnishes: **apple slices, orange slices, orange zest, salad greens**
1¼	cups **orange marmalade**		

Ham is a perennial favorite that's easy to prepare. It's also a smart choice because it yields plenty of leftovers.

1. Preheat oven to 350°. Remove skin from ham, and trim fat to ¼-inch thickness. Make ¼-inch-deep cuts in a diamond pattern, and insert cloves at 1-inch intervals. Place ham in an aluminum foil–lined 13- x 9-inch pan.

2. Stir together soft drink and next 3 ingredients until smooth. Pour mixture evenly over ham.

3. Bake at 350° on lower oven rack 2 hours and 30 minutes, basting with pan juices every 20 minutes. Remove ham; let stand 15 minutes before serving. Garnish, if desired.

Note: We tested with Orangina Sparkling Citrus Beverage.

Garlic-Herb Roasted Chicken

makes 4 to 6 servings ☆ prep: 10 min. ☆ cook: 1 hr., 15 min. ☆ stand: 10 min.

Add additional moistness and flavor by replacing the wire roasting rack with a flavorful and colorful rack of carrots and celery ribs. Tuck in a few sprigs of fresh herbs, some unpeeled whole shallots, and apple slices.

3	**garlic cloves,** minced	1	tsp. chopped **fresh sage**
2	tsp. chopped **fresh thyme**	1	tsp. **salt**
2	tsp. chopped **fresh rosemary**	¾	tsp. freshly **ground pepper**
2	tsp. chopped **fresh parsley**	1	(4- to 5-lb.) **whole chicken**

1. Preheat oven to 450°. Stir together first 7 ingredients.

2. If applicable, remove giblets from chicken, and reserve for another use. Rinse chicken, and pat dry. Gently loosen and lift skin from breast and drumsticks with fingers. (Do not totally detach skin.) Rub herb mixture underneath skin. Carefully replace skin. Place chicken, breast side up, on a lightly greased wire rack in a lightly greased shallow roasting pan. Tie ends of legs together with string; tuck wing tips under.

3. Bake at 450° for 30 minutes. Reduce heat to 350°, and bake 45 minutes or until a meat thermometer inserted in thigh registers 180°, covering loosely with aluminum foil to prevent excessive browning, if necessary. Let chicken stand, covered, 10 minutes before slicing.

Chicken Dijon

makes 6 servings ☆ prep: 25 min. ☆ cook: 30 min.

6	skinned and boned **chicken breasts** (about 2 lb.)	1	medium-size **sweet onion,** diced
½	tsp. **salt**	1	(14½-oz.) can **chicken broth**
½	tsp. **pepper**	3	Tbsp. **all-purpose flour**
3	Tbsp. **butter**	3	Tbsp. **Dijon mustard**
1	medium-size **red bell pepper,** cut into thin strips		

With this recipe you can have a crowd-pleasing meal on the table in just under an hour.

1. Sprinkle chicken with salt and pepper.

2. Melt butter in a large skillet over medium-high heat; add chicken, and cook 3 to 4 minutes on each side or until golden brown. Remove chicken from skillet; add bell pepper and onion, and cook, stirring often, 4 to 5 minutes or until vegetables are tender. Return chicken to skillet.

3. Whisk together broth and next 2 ingredients, and pour over chicken. Cover, reduce heat to low, and simmer 20 minutes or until chicken is done.

Note: For an easy side: Prepare frozen mashed sweet potatoes according to package directions. Stir in chopped fresh sage, butter, and salt and pepper to taste.

Oven Chicken Risotto

makes 6 servings ☆ prep: 20 min. ☆ cook: 40 min.

2   Tbsp. **butter**

2½ cups **chicken broth**

1   cup uncooked **Arborio rice** (short-grain)

½   small **onion,** diced

½   tsp. **salt**

2   cups chopped **deli-roasted chicken**

1   (8-oz.) package fresh **mozzarella cheese,** cut into ½-inch cubes

1   cup **cherry** or **grape tomatoes,** halved

¼   cup shredded **fresh basil**

This baked version allows you to enjoy creamy risotto without the constant stirring required by the traditional method.

1. Preheat oven to 400°. Place butter in a 13- x 9-inch baking dish; bake 5 minutes or until melted. Stir in broth and next 3 ingredients.

2. Bake, covered, at 400° for 35 minutes. Remove from oven. Fluff rice with a fork. Stir in chicken, mozzarella, and tomatoes; sprinkle with shredded basil. Serve immediately.

Note: For an easy side: Cook 1 lb. tiny green beans (haricots verts) in boiling salted water until crisp-tender; drain and sprinkle with freshly cracked pepper. Add hot buttered rolls, if desired, and dinner is served.

Kentucky Hot Brown Tart

makes 6 to 8 servings ☆ prep: 30 min. ☆ cook: 1 hr. ☆ cool: 30 min.

Inspired by the flavors of the traditional open-faced sandwich, this tart is ideal for your next Derby party or a casual week-night supper.

1 (14.1-oz.) package **refrigerated piecrusts**

1½ cups chopped **cooked turkey**

2 cups (8 oz.) shredded **white Cheddar cheese**

¼ cup finely chopped **fresh chives**

6 **bacon slices**, cooked and crumbled

1½ cups **half-and-half**

4 large **eggs**

½ tsp. **salt**

¼ tsp. freshly ground **pepper**

2 **plum tomatoes**, cut into ¼-inch-thick slices

½ cup freshly grated **Parmesan cheese**

1. Preheat oven to 425°. Unroll piecrusts; stack on a lightly greased surface. Roll stacked piecrusts into a 12-inch circle. Fit piecrust into a 10-inch deep-dish tart pan with removable bottom; press into fluted edges. Trim off excess piecrust along edges. Line piecrust with aluminum foil or parchment paper, and fill with pie weights or dried beans. Place pan on a foil-lined baking sheet. Bake 12 minutes. Remove weights and foil from piecrust, and bake 8 more minutes. Cool completely on baking sheet on a wire rack (about 15 minutes). Reduce oven temperature to 350°.

2. Layer turkey and next 3 ingredients in tart shell on baking sheet.

3. Whisk together half-and-half and next 3 ingredients; pour over turkey.

4. Bake at 350° for 30 to 40 minutes or until set.

5. Place tomatoes in a single layer on paper towels; press tomatoes lightly with paper towels. Arrange over top of tart, and sprinkle with Parmesan cheese. Bake 10 to 15 minutes or until cheese is melted. Cool on baking sheet on wire rack 15 minutes.

Southern-Style Fish Tacos

makes 4 servings ☆ prep: 20 min. ☆ cook: 2 min. per batch

3   large **limes**, divided
4   (6-oz.) **catfish fillets**, cut into
     1-inch-thick strips
1½   cups **yellow cornmeal**
2   Tbsp. **dried parsley flakes**
2   Tbsp. **paprika**
2   tsp. **ground red pepper**
2   tsp. **lemon pepper**
2   tsp. **salt**
1   tsp. **garlic powder**
Canola oil
8   (6-inch) **corn** or **flour tortillas,**
     warmed

1   cup thinly shredded **green**
     cabbage
1   cup thinly shredded **red**
     cabbage
Refrigerated creamy Ranch
     dressing
Bottled salsa
Toppings: **avocado slices,**
     seeded and diced tomatoes,
     chopped fresh cilantro

These tacos are as flavorful as they are colorful.

1. Squeeze juice of 1 lime over fish. Combine cornmeal and next 6 ingredients in a large zip-top plastic freezer bag. Pat fish dry with paper towels, and place in bag, shaking to coat.

2. Pour oil to a depth of 1½ inches in a large deep skillet; heat to 325°. Fry catfish, in batches, in hot oil 2 to 3 minutes or until crispy and golden brown. Drain on paper towels.

3. Place catfish in warmed tortillas; top evenly with cabbage, desired amount of salad dressing, salsa, and toppings. Cut remaining 2 limes into wedges, and serve with tacos.

**Classic Parmesan Scalloped
Potatoes, page 200**

Chapter 6

SIDE DISHES

Classic Parmesan Scalloped Potatoes

makes 8 to 10 servings ☆ prep: 20 min. ☆ cook: 45 min. ☆ stand: 10 min.
pictured on page 198

Gently stirring twice while baking promotes even cooking and creaminess in this dish. Pull out of the oven, stir once more, then sprinkle with cheese, and continue baking without stirring for a casserole that's golden brown on top.

2 lb. **Yukon gold potatoes,** peeled and thinly sliced
3 cups **whipping cream**
¼ cup chopped **fresh flat-leaf parsley**
2 **garlic cloves,** chopped
1½ tsp. **salt**
¼ tsp. freshly ground **pepper**
½ cup grated **Parmesan cheese**

1. Preheat oven to 400°. Layer potatoes in a 13- x 9-inch or 3-qt. baking dish.

2. Stir together cream and next 4 ingredients in a large bowl. Pour cream mixture over potatoes.

3. Bake at 400° for 30 minutes, stirring gently every 10 minutes. Sprinkle with cheese; bake 15 to 20 minutes or until bubbly and golden brown. Let stand on a wire rack 10 minutes before serving.

variation

Gruyère Scalloped Potatoes: Substitute finely shredded Gruyère cheese for Parmesan. Reduce parsley to 2 Tbsp. and salt to 1 tsp. Prepare recipe as directed, stirring 1 tsp. freshly ground Italian seasoning into cream mixture in Step 2.

Note: We tested with McCormick Italian Herb Seasoning Grinder.

Browned Butter Mashed Potatoes

makes 6 to 8 servings ☆ prep: 15 min. ☆ cook: 29 min.

¾ cup **butter**

4 lb. **Yukon gold potatoes,** peeled and cut into 2-inch pieces

1 Tbsp. **salt,** divided

¾ cup **buttermilk**

½ cup **milk**

¼ tsp. **pepper**

Garnishes: **fresh parsley, rosemary, and thyme sprigs**

Also, try tossing browned butter with steamed vegetables, or drizzle it over warm, crusty French bread.

1. Cook butter in a 2-qt. heavy saucepan over medium heat, stirring constantly, 6 to 8 minutes or just until butter begins to turn golden brown. Immediately remove pan from heat, and pour butter into a small bowl. (Butter will continue to darken if left in saucepan.) Remove and reserve 1 to 2 Tbsp. browned butter.

2. Bring potatoes, 2 tsp. salt, and water to cover to a boil in a large Dutch oven over medium-high heat; boil 20 minutes or until tender. Drain. Reduce heat to low. Return potatoes to Dutch oven, and cook, stirring occasionally, 3 to 5 minutes or until potatoes are dry.

3. Mash potatoes with a potato masher to desired consistency. Stir in remaining browned butter, buttermilk, milk, pepper, and remaining 1 tsp. salt, stirring just until blended.

4. Transfer to a serving dish. Drizzle with reserved 1 to 2 Tbsp. browned butter. Garnish, if desired.

Corn Pudding

makes 6 to 8 servings ☆ prep: 18 min. ☆ cook: 42 min. ☆ stand: 5 min.

9	ears **fresh corn**	2	Tbsp. **sugar**
4	large **eggs,** beaten	2	Tbsp. **all-purpose flour**
½	cup **half-and-half**	1	Tbsp. **butter,** melted
1½	tsp. **baking powder**	⅛	tsp. freshly ground **pepper**
⅓	cup **butter**		

Creamed corn baked in custard is a traditional dish worth preserving.

1. Remove and discard husks and silks from corn. Cut off tips of corn kernels into a bowl, and scrape milk and remaining pulp from cob with a paring knife to measure 3 to 4 cups total. Set corn aside.

2. Combine eggs, half-and-half, and baking powder, stirring well with a wire whisk.

3. Preheat oven to 350°. Melt ⅓ cup butter in a large saucepan over low heat; add sugar and flour, stirring until smooth. Remove from heat; gradually add egg mixture, whisking constantly until smooth. Stir in reserved corn.

4. Pour corn mixture into a greased 1- or 1½-quart baking dish.

5. Bake, uncovered, at 350° for 40 to 45 minutes or until pudding is set. Drizzle pudding with 1 Tbsp. butter; sprinkle with pepper.

6. Broil 5½ inches from heat 2 minutes or until golden. Let stand 5 minutes before serving.

Grits and Greens

makes 6 to 8 servings ☆ prep: 15 min. ☆ cook: 35 min.

Two classic Southern foods come together in this old-fashioned yet trendy recipe. Stir them together, or spoon them side by side on each plate. And don't forget the ham garnish; sauté it briefly for the best flavor.

1 cup **whipping cream**
4 cups **chicken broth,** divided
1 cup uncooked **stone-ground grits**
¼ to ½ cup **milk** or **chicken broth** (optional)
1 lb. **fresh collard greens**

¼ cup **butter**
1 to 1½ cups (4 to 6 oz.) freshly grated **Parmesan cheese**
¼ to ½ tsp. freshly ground **pepper**
Garnish: cubed **cooked ham** or chopped **cooked bacon**

1. Combine whipping cream and 3 cups chicken broth in a large saucepan. Bring to a boil, and gradually stir in grits.

2. Cook over medium heat until mixture returns to a boil; cover, reduce heat, and simmer 25 to 30 minutes, stirring often. Gradually add milk or more chicken broth, if necessary, for desired consistency.

3. Remove and discard stems and any discolored spots from greens. Wash greens thoroughly; drain and cut into ½-inch strips.

4. Combine greens and remaining 1 cup chicken broth in a large skillet; bring to a boil. Cover, reduce heat, and simmer 10 to 20 minutes or until greens are tender.

5. Add butter, cheese, and pepper to grits, stirring until butter and cheese are melted. Stir in greens, if desired; cook just until thoroughly heated, or serve grits and greens side by side on each plate. Garnish, if desired.

Crumb-Topped Spinach Casserole

makes 8 to 10 servings ☆ prep: 13 min. ☆ cook: 38 min.

This quick, cheesy side, with its crunchy browned topping, can be ready to bake in just over the time it takes to preheat the oven. It's so good, it'll persuade even the kids to eat spinach.

2 Tbsp. **butter**
1 medium **onion,** chopped
2 **garlic cloves,** minced
4 (10-oz.) packages **frozen chopped spinach,** thawed
1 (8-oz.) package **cream cheese,** softened
2 Tbsp. **all-purpose flour**
2 large **eggs**
½ tsp. **salt**
¼ tsp. **pepper**
1 cup **milk**
1 (8-oz.) package shredded **Cheddar cheese**
1 cup **Italian-seasoned Japanese breadcrumbs (panko)** or **homemade breadcrumbs**
3 to 4 Tbsp. **butter,** melted

1. Preheat oven to 350°. Melt 2 Tbsp. butter in a large nonstick skillet over medium heat. Add onion and garlic, and sauté 8 minutes or until tender.

2. Meanwhile, drain spinach well, pressing between paper towels to remove excess moisture.

3. Stir together cream cheese and flour in a large bowl until smooth. Whisk in eggs, salt, and pepper. Gradually whisk in milk until blended. Add sautéed onion mixture, spinach, and Cheddar cheese, stirring until blended. Spoon into a lightly greased 11- x 7-inch baking dish.

4. Combine breadcrumbs and 3 to 4 Tbsp. butter in a small bowl; toss well. Sprinkle over casserole.

5. Bake, uncovered, at 350° for 30 to 35 minutes or until thoroughly heated and breadcrumbs are browned.

Note: To make individual spinach casseroles, spoon spinach mixture into 8 (8-oz.) lightly greased ramekins; top each with buttered breadcrumbs. Bake, uncovered, at 375° for 25 to 30 minutes or until browned. (We found that a slightly higher temperature produced better results for individual casseroles.)

Creamy Baked Sweet Onions

makes 4 servings ☆ prep: 30 min. ☆ cook: 34 min.

2 (10-oz.) packages **cipollini boiler onions, unpeeled***
2 Tbsp. **butter**
2 Tbsp. **all-purpose flour**
1½ cups **milk**
1½ cups (6 oz.) shredded **sharp white Cheddar cheese**
1 tsp. **hot sauce**
¼ tsp. **salt**
⅛ tsp. ground **white pepper**
¼ cup crushed **round buttery crackers**
1 Tbsp. melted **butter**

This dish has everything you expect in a good casserole—a creamy, rich base with a crispy, crunchy topping.

1. Preheat oven to 350°. Cook onions in a large saucepan in boiling water to cover 5 to 7 minutes. Drain, cool slightly, and peel. Place in a lightly greased 8-inch square baking dish.

2. Melt 2 Tbsp. butter in a heavy saucepan over medium heat; whisk in flour until smooth, and cook, whisking constantly, 1 minute. Gradually whisk in milk, and cook, whisking constantly, 1 minute or until thickened and bubbly. Add cheese, hot sauce, salt, and ground white pepper, and whisk 2 minutes or until cheese is melted. Pour mixture over onions in dish.

3. Stir together crushed crackers and 1 Tbsp. melted butter; sprinkle over top of casserole.

4. Bake at 350° for 25 to 30 minutes or until bubbly.

* 20 oz. sweet onions, peeled and cut into wedges, may be substituted. Omit boiling onions in Step 1; peel and place in baking dish as directed.

Balsamic Root Vegetables

makes 6 to 8 servings ☆ prep: 25 min. ☆ cook: 4 hr.

For a delicious twist, top with a sprinkling of cooked and crumbled bacon just before serving.

1½ lb. **sweet potatoes**
1 lb. **parsnips**
1 lb. **carrots**
2 large **red onions**, coarsely chopped
¾ cup **sweetened dried cranberries**

1 Tbsp. **light brown sugar**
3 Tbsp. **olive oil**
2 Tbsp. **balsamic vinegar**
1 tsp. **salt**
½ tsp. freshly ground **pepper**
⅓ cup chopped **fresh flat-leaf parsley**

1. Peel first 3 ingredients, and cut into 1½-inch pieces. Combine parsnips, carrots, onions, and cranberries in a lightly greased 6-qt. slow cooker; layer sweet potatoes over top.

2. Whisk together sugar and next 4 ingredients in a small bowl; pour over vegetable mixture. (Do not stir.)

3. Cover and cook on HIGH 4 to 5 hours or until vegetables are tender. Toss with parsley just before serving.

Okra and Tomatoes

makes 8 servings ☆ prep: 25 min. ☆ cook: 20 min.

4	bacon slices		1	tsp. salt
1	large sweet onion, chopped		1	tsp. pepper
3	large tomatoes, chopped		1	garlic clove, minced
1	lb. fresh okra, chopped		**Hot cooked rice**	

1. Cook bacon in a large skillet or Dutch oven over medium heat until crisp. Remove and crumble bacon; reserve 2 Tbsp. drippings in skillet.

2. Sauté onion in hot drippings over medium-high heat 5 minutes or until tender. Stir in tomatoes and next 4 ingredients. Reduce heat, and cook, stirring often, 10 minutes or until okra is tender. Serve over rice, and sprinkle with bacon.

ingredient spotlight

First brought to the area by West African slaves, okra is a staple of Lowcountry cuisine, which stretches from the coast of North Carolina to north Florida.

Juicy, summer-ripe tomatoes make this dish shine. You can use a large can of San Marzano tomatoes, chopped, as an out-of-season option.

Fried Green Tomatoes

makes 6 to 8 servings ☆ prep: 15 min. ☆ cook: 6 min. per batch

4	large **green tomatoes**	1	cup **all-purpose flour**	
1½	cups **buttermilk**	1	cup **self-rising cornmeal mix**	
1	Tbsp. **salt**	3	cups **vegetable oil**	
1	tsp. **pepper**	**Salt** to taste		

Dipped in buttermilk and then in a flour-and-cornmeal coating before frying, these tomatoes come out hot, crisp, and juicy.

1. Cut tomatoes into ¼- to ⅓-inch-thick slices; place in a shallow dish. Pour buttermilk over tomatoes. Sprinkle with salt and pepper.

2. Combine flour and cornmeal in a shallow dish or pie plate. Dredge tomato slices in flour mixture.

3. Fry tomatoes, in batches, in hot oil in a large cast-iron skillet over medium heat 3 minutes on each side or until golden. Drain tomatoes on paper towels. Sprinkle with salt to taste.

variation

Try these crunchy tomatoes in place of fresh tomatoes in a BLT for a special upgrade.

Lemon-Garlic Green Beans

makes 8 servings ☆ prep: 15 min. ☆ cook: 6 min.

Lemon juice and basil create a fresh flavor that makes these green beans worthy of a special occasion.

1½ lb. **fresh haricots verts** (tiny green beans), trimmed
2 tsp. **salt,** divided
3 **garlic cloves,** minced
3 **shallots,** sliced
2 Tbsp. **olive oil**

¼ cup chopped **fresh basil**
3 Tbsp. **fresh lemon juice**
¼ tsp. **pepper**
Garnishes: **lemon zest, fresh basil leaves**

1. Cook beans with 1 tsp. salt in boiling water to cover 4 to 5 minutes or until crisp-tender; drain. Plunge beans into ice water to stop the cooking process; drain.

2. Cook garlic and shallots in hot oil in a large nonstick skillet over medium heat 2 minutes or until just golden brown; remove from heat. Stir in basil, next 2 ingredients, and remaining 1 tsp. salt. Add green beans, and toss to coat. Garnish, if desired.

Caramelized Onion–and-Pecan Brussels Sprouts

makes 8 servings ☆ prep: 15 min. ☆ chill: 8 hr. ☆ cook: 23 min.

Even the pickiest of eaters will eat their Brussels sprouts when combined with sweet caramelized onions and crunchy pecans.

1	large **onion**	1	cup **pecan pieces**
1	lb. **Brussels sprouts**	1	tsp. **salt**
¼	cup **butter**	½	tsp. **pepper**

1. Cut onion in half, and thinly slice. Cut Brussels sprouts in half, and cut each half crosswise into thin slices. Place vegetables in separate plastic bags; seal and chill 8 hours.

2. Melt butter in a large heavy skillet over medium-high heat; add pecans, and sauté 5 minutes or until toasted and fragrant. Remove pecans from skillet. Add onion to skillet; cook, stirring often, 15 minutes or until caramel-colored. Add pecans and Brussels sprouts, and cook 3 minutes or until heated. Sprinkle with salt and pepper.

Strawberry-Pineapple Iceberg Wedges

makes 6 servings ☆ prep: 30 min.

1   (16-oz.) package **fresh strawberries**, hulled
½   medium **pineapple**, peeled and cored
½   medium **honeydew melon**
¼   small **cantaloupe**

2   Tbsp. chopped **fresh mint**
1   head **iceberg lettuce**, cored and cut into 6 wedges
Kosher salt and freshly ground **pepper** to taste
Yogurt–Poppy Seed Dressing

Look for seeded melon halves in the produce department to save a little time.

1. Cut first 4 ingredients into ¼-inch pieces (about 2 cups each cubed strawberries, pineapple, and honeydew melon and 1 cup cubed cantaloupe). Toss with mint.

2. Arrange 1 lettuce wedge on each of 6 serving plates. Top evenly with fruit mixture. Sprinkle with salt and pepper to taste. Drizzle with Yogurt–Poppy Seed Dressing.

Yogurt–Poppy Seed Dressing

makes 1 cup ☆ prep: 10 min.

1   cup **plain Greek or plain yogurt**
2   Tbsp. **honey**

2   Tbsp. **fresh lemon juice**
1   tsp. **poppy seeds**

Yogurt and honey replace the oil and sugar typically found in this classic for a healthful, here-and-now dressing. We prefer Greek yogurt for its thick consistency and rich flavor, but plain yogurt can be substituted for a thinner dressing.

1. Whisk together all ingredients in a small bowl. Store in an airtight container in refrigerator up to 5 days.

Spinach-Apple Salad With Maple-Cider Vinaigrette

makes 8 servings ☆ prep: 20 min. ☆ cook: 10 min. ☆ cool: 20 min.

1   (10-oz.) package **fresh baby spinach**
1   **Gala apple,** thinly sliced
1   small **red onion,** thinly sliced
1   (4-oz.) package **crumbled goat cheese**
    Maple-Cider Vinaigrette
    Sugared Curried Pecans

1. Combine spinach and next 3 ingredients in a bowl. Drizzle with desired amount of Maple-Cider Vinaigrette; toss to coat. Sprinkle with Sugared Candied Pecans. Serve salad with any remaining vinaigrette.

Maple-Cider Vinaigrette

⅓   cup **cider vinegar**
2   Tbsp. **pure maple syrup**
1   Tbsp. **Dijon mustard**
¼   tsp. **kosher salt**
¼   tsp. **pepper**
⅔   cup **olive oil**

1. Whisk together cider vinegar and next 4 ingredients. Gradually whisk in oil until well blended.

Sugared Curried Pecans

1 (6-oz.) package **pecan halves**
2 Tbsp. **butter,** melted
3 Tbsp. **sugar**
¼ tsp. ground **ginger**

⅛ tsp. **curry powder**
⅛ tsp. **kosher salt**
⅛ tsp. **ground red pepper**

1. Preheat oven to 350°. Toss pecans in butter. Stir together sugar and next 4 ingredients in a bowl; add pecans, tossing to coat. Spread in a single layer in a nonstick aluminum foil–lined pan. Bake 10 to 13 minutes or until lightly browned and toasted. Cool in pan on a wire rack 20 minutes; separate pecans with a fork.

make ahead

Pecans may be made up to 1 week ahead. Store in an airtight container. Vinaigrette may be made up to 3 days ahead. Cover and chill until ready to serve.

Grilled Peach-and-Mozzarella Salad

makes 4 servings ☆ prep: 25 min. ☆ cook: 6 min.

5	peaches (not white)	1½	Tbsp. **tequila** (optional)
3	**green onions**, sliced	⅓	cup **olive oil**
¼	cup chopped **fresh cilantro**		**Vegetable cooking spray**
3	Tbsp. **honey**	1	(6-oz.) package **watercress**
1	tsp. **salt**		or **baby arugula**
1	tsp. **lime zest**	¾	lb. **fresh mozzarella**, cut into
½	cup **fresh lime juice**		16 (¼-inch) slices
¾	tsp. **ground cumin**		Garnish: **fresh cilantro sprigs**
¾	tsp. **chili powder**		

We found traditional peaches work best in this dish. White peaches have more sugar and water and don't hold up as well on the grill. As the seasons change, consider substituting heirloom tomatoes, plums, and other soft fruits for the peaches.

1. Peel and chop 1 peach. Cut remaining 4 peaches into 28 (¼-inch-thick) rounds, cutting through stem and bottom ends. (Cut peaches inward from sides, cutting each side just until you reach the pit. Discard pits.) Process chopped peach, green onions, next 7 ingredients, and, if desired, tequila in a food processor 10 to 15 seconds or until smooth. Add oil, and pulse 3 or 4 times or until thoroughly combined.

2. Coat cold cooking grate of grill with cooking spray, and place on grill. Preheat grill to medium-high heat (350° to 400°). Brush both sides of peach rounds with ⅓ cup peach dressing. Grill peach rounds, covered with grill lid, 3 to 5 minutes on each side or until grill marks appear.

3. Arrange watercress evenly on 4 plates. Alternately layer 4 grilled peach rounds and 4 cheese slices over watercress on each plate. Top each with 3 more peach rounds. Drizzle with remaining peach dressing. Garnish, if desired.

Note: You can also use a grill pan to get beautiful grill marks on the peaches.

Tomato-and-Watermelon Salad

makes 4 to 6 servings ☆ prep: 20 min. ☆ stand: 15 min. ☆ chill: 2 hr.

Combine sweet, juicy watermelon chunks with fresh tomato, onion, and red wine vinaigrette for a salad that's the essence of summer.

5 cups (¾-inch) seeded **watermelon cubes**

1½ lb. ripe **tomatoes,** cut into ¾-inch cubes

3 tsp. **sugar**

½ tsp. **salt**

1 small **red onion,** quartered and thinly sliced

½ cup **red wine vinegar**

¼ cup **extra-virgin olive oil**

Romaine lettuce leaves (optional)

Cracked black pepper to taste

1. Combine watermelon and tomatoes in a large bowl; sprinkle with sugar and salt, tossing to coat. Let stand 15 minutes.

2. Stir in onion, vinegar, and oil. Cover and chill 2 hours. Serve chilled with lettuce leaves, if desired. Sprinkle with cracked black pepper to taste.

Peanutty Coleslaw

makes 6 servings ☆ prep: 15 min. ☆ chill: 1 hr.

½ cup chopped **fresh cilantro**
¼ cup chopped **green onions**
3 Tbsp. **white vinegar**
1 Tbsp. **sesame oil**
2 Tbsp. **mayonnaise**
1 tsp. **sugar**
1 tsp. grated **fresh ginger**

2 tsp. **wasabi paste**
½ tsp. **salt**
½ tsp. **pepper**
1 (16-oz.) package shredded **coleslaw mix**
¾ cup lightly salted **peanuts**

Wasabi paste can be purchased in the Asian section of most supermarkets. If you prefer a creamy coleslaw, double the amount of dressing.

1. Whisk together first 10 ingredients in a large bowl; add coleslaw mix, stirring to coat. Cover and chill 1 hour; stir in peanuts just before serving.

twist on tradition

Lightly dressed and less creamy than more traditional versions, this coleslaw is the perfect crunchy, zesty side for a summer gathering.

Hot Bacon Potato Salad with Green Beans

makes 8 servings ☆ prep: 10 min. ☆ cook: 20 min.

3	lb. **fingerling potatoes**, cut in half	1½	tsp. **salt**	
1	(8-oz.) package **haricots verts** (tiny green beans)	1	tsp. **pepper**	
½	cup **white wine vinegar**	½	cup **olive oil**	
1	**shallot,** minced	2	Tbsp. chopped **fresh dill**	
3	Tbsp. **honey**	¼	cup coarsely chopped **fresh parsley**	
1	Tbsp. **Dijon mustard**	4	fully cooked **bacon slices,** chopped	

Use some purple fingerling potatoes for a stunning appearance.

1. Bring potatoes and water to cover to a boil in a large Dutch oven over medium-high heat, and cook 20 minutes or until tender. Drain.

2. Meanwhile, cook haricots verts in boiling water to cover in a medium saucepan 3 to 4 minutes or until crisp-tender. Plunge in ice water to stop the cooking process; drain.

3. Whisk together vinegar and next 5 ingredients in a medium bowl. Add oil in a slow, steady stream, whisking constantly, until smooth.

4. Pour vinegar mixture over potatoes. Just before serving, add haricots verts, dill, and parsley, and toss gently until blended. Sprinkle with bacon. Serve immediately, or cover and chill until ready to serve.

Broccoli, Grape, and Pasta Salad

makes 6 to 8 servings ☆ prep: 15 min. ☆ cook: 15 min. ☆ chill: 3 hr.

If you're a broccoli salad fan, you'll love the combination of these colorful ingredients. Cook the pasta al dente so it's firm enough to hold its own when tossed with the tangy-sweet salad dressing.

1	cup chopped **pecans**
½	(16-oz.) package **farfalle (bow-tie) pasta**
1	lb. **fresh broccoli**
1	cup **mayonnaise**
⅓	cup **sugar**
⅓	cup diced **red onion**
⅓	cup **red wine vinegar**
1	tsp. **salt**
2	cups **seedless red grapes,** halved
8	cooked **bacon slices,** crumbled

1. Preheat oven to 350°. Bake pecans in a single layer in a shallow pan 5 to 7 minutes or until lightly toasted and fragrant, stirring halfway through.

2. Prepare pasta according to package directions.

3. Meanwhile, cut broccoli florets from stems, and separate florets into small pieces using tip of a paring knife. Peel away tough outer layer of stems, and finely chop stems.

4. Whisk together mayonnaise and next 4 ingredients in a large bowl; add broccoli, hot cooked pasta, and grapes, and stir to coat. Cover and chill 3 hours. Stir bacon and pecans into salad just before serving.

Triple-Decker Strawberry Cake, page 236

Chapter 7

SWEET ENDINGS

Triple-Decker Strawberry Cake

makes 12 servings ☆ prep: 25 min. ☆ cook: 23 min. ☆ cool: 1 hr., 10 min.
pictured on page 234

This cake from Anne Byrn, aka The Cake Mix Doctor, is so good no one will know it's not made from scratch. We doubled the frosting called for in Anne's original recipe to add extra richness.

1 (18.25-oz.) package white cake mix
1 (3-oz.) package strawberry gelatin
4 large eggs
½ cup sugar
½ cup finely chopped fresh strawberries
½ cup milk
½ cup vegetable oil
⅓ cup all-purpose flour
Strawberry Buttercream Frosting
Garnish: whole and halved strawberries

1. Preheat oven to 350°. Beat cake mix and next 7 ingredients at low speed with an electric mixer 1 minute. Scrape down sides, and beat at medium speed 2 more minutes, stopping to scrape down sides as needed. (Strawberries should be well blended.)

2. Pour batter into 3 greased and floured 9-inch round cake pans.

3. Bake at 350° for 23 minutes or until cakes spring back when pressed lightly with a finger. Let cool in pans on wire racks 10 minutes. Remove from pans, and cool completely (about 1 hour).

4. Spread Strawberry Buttercream Frosting between layers and on top and sides of cake. Garnish, if desired. Serve immediately, or chill up to 1 week.

Note: We tested with Betty Crocker SuperMoist Cake Mix, White.

Strawberry Buttercream Frosting

makes 2½ cups ☆ prep: 10 min.

1 cup butter, softened
1 (32-oz.) package powdered sugar, sifted
1 cup finely chopped fresh strawberries

1. Beat butter at medium speed with an electric mixer until fluffy (about 20 seconds). Add sugar and strawberries, beating at low speed until creamy. (Add more sugar if frosting is too thin, or add strawberries if too thick.)

Shortcut Carrot Cake

makes 12 servings ☆ prep: 15 min. ☆ cook: 18 min. ☆ cool: 10 min.
chill: 2 hr.

1	(26.5-oz.) package **cinnamon streusel coffee cake mix**	½	cup chopped **pecans**, toasted
3	large **eggs**	1	cup **sweetened flaked coconut**
⅓	cup **vegetable oil**	2	Tbsp. **orange juice**
3	large **carrots**, finely grated		**Cream Cheese Frosting**

If you have a sweet tooth but you're short on time, this cake takes just about 45 minutes to prepare, bake, and frost.

1. Preheat oven to 350°. Grease 3 (8-inch) round cake pans. Line with wax paper; grease and flour pans.

2. Combine cake mix and streusel packet in a mixing bowl, reserving glaze packet. Add eggs, 1¼ cups water, and oil; beat at medium speed with an electric mixer 2 minutes. Stir in carrots, pecans, and coconut. Pour batter evenly into prepared pans.

3. Bake at 350° for 18 to 20 minutes. Cool in pans on wire racks 10 minutes. Remove from pans; place on racks.

4. Stir together reserved glaze and juice; brush evenly over warm cake layers. Cool completely on wire racks.

5. Spread Cream Cheese Frosting between layers and on top and sides of cake. Chill frosted cake at least 2 hours.

Cream Cheese Frosting

makes 5 cups ☆ prep: 10 min.

1	(8-oz.) package **cream cheese,** softened	¾	cup **butter,** softened
		7	cups **powdered sugar**
1	(3-oz.) package **cream cheese,** softened	1	Tbsp. **vanilla extract**
		3	to 4 Tbsp. **milk**

1. Beat cream cheese and butter at medium speed with an electric mixer until fluffy; gradually add powdered sugar, beating well. Stir in vanilla. Add milk, 1 Tbsp. at a time, until frosting reaches desired consistency.

Chocolate Turtle Cake

makes 12 servings ☆ prep: 40 min. ☆ cook: 30 min. ☆ other: 1 hr., 10 min.

Unsweetened cocoa
1   (18.25-oz.) package **devil's food cake mix**
1   (3.9-oz.) package **chocolate instant pudding mix**
3   large **eggs**
1¼ cups **milk**
1   cup **canola oil**
2   tsp. **vanilla extract**
1   tsp. **chocolate extract**
1   tsp. **instant coffee granules**
1   (6-oz.) package **semisweet chocolate morsels**

1   cup chopped **pecans**
1   (16-oz.) container **ready-to-spread cream cheese frosting**
½   cup canned **dulce de leche**
2   (7-oz.) packages **turtle candies**
1   (16-oz.) can **ready-to-spread chocolate fudge frosting**
1   (12-oz.) jar **dulce de leche ice cream topping**
¼   cup **pecan halves**, toasted

The jarred dulce de leche ice cream topping is perfect to drizzle over the finished cake. Find it in the supermarket with other ice cream toppings.

1. Preheat oven to 350°. Grease 2 (9-inch) round cake pans, and dust with cocoa. Set aside.

2. Beat cake mix and next 7 ingredients at low speed with an electric mixer 1 minute; beat at medium speed 2 minutes. Fold in chocolate morsels and chopped pecans. Pour batter into prepared pans.

3. Bake at 350° for 30 to 32 minutes or until a wooden pick inserted in center comes out clean. Cool in pans on wire racks 10 minutes. Remove from pans to wire racks, and cool completely. Wrap and chill cake layers at least 1 hour.

4. Whisk together cream cheese frosting and canned dulce de leche in a small bowl until well blended. Set aside. Cut 6 turtle candies in half, and set aside for garnish. Dice remaining turtle candies.

5. Using a serrated knife, slice cake layers in half horizontally to make 4 layers. Place 1 layer, cut side up, on cake plate. Spread with ½ cup cream cheese frosting mixture; sprinkle with one-third diced turtle candies. Repeat procedure twice. Place final cake layer on top of cake, cut side down. Spread chocolate fudge frosting on top and sides of cake. Cover and chill in refrigerator until ready to serve. Just before serving, drizzle dulce de leche ice cream topping over top of cake. Garnish with remaining halved turtle candies and pecan halves. Store in refrigerator.

Skillet Pineapple Upside-Down Cake

makes 8 to 10 servings ☆ prep: 20 min. ☆ cook: 45 min. ☆ cool: 30 min.

¼ cup **butter**

⅔ cup firmly packed **light** or **dark brown sugar**

1 (20-oz.) can **pineapple slices,** undrained

8 **maraschino cherries**

2 large **eggs,** separated

¾ cup granulated **sugar**

¾ cup **all-purpose flour**

⅛ tsp. **salt**

½ tsp. **baking powder**

Whipped cream or **vanilla ice cream** (optional)

1. Preheat oven to 325°. Melt butter in a 9-inch cast-iron skillet. Spread brown sugar evenly over bottom of skillet. Drain pineapple, reserving ¼ cup juice; set juice aside. Arrange pineapple slices in a single layer over brown sugar mixture, and place a cherry in center of each pineapple ring; set skillet aside.

2. Beat egg yolks at medium speed with an electric mixer until thick and pale; gradually add granulated sugar, beating well.

3. Heat reserved pineapple juice in a small saucepan over low heat. Gradually add juice mixture to yolk mixture, beating until blended.

4. Combine flour, salt, and baking powder; add dry ingredients to yolk mixture, beating at low speed with mixer until blended.

5. Beat egg whites until stiff peaks form; fold egg whites into batter. Spoon batter evenly over pineapple slices.

6. Bake at 325° for 45 to 50 minutes. Cool cake in skillet 30 minutes; invert cake onto a serving plate. Serve warm or cold with whipped cream or ice cream, if desired.

variation

Express Pineapple Upside-Down Cake: Follow original recipe directions for first 4 ingredients. Substitute 1 (9-oz.) package golden yellow cake mix for next 5 ingredients. Prepare cake mix according to package directions, substituting ½ cup pineapple juice for ½ cup water. Spoon batter over prepared pineapple slices as directed. Bake at 350° for 20 to 25 minutes or until a wooden pick inserted in center comes out clean.

Note: We tested with Jiffy Golden Yellow Cake Mix.

Million-Dollar Pound Cake

makes 10 to 12 servings ☆ prep: 20 min. ☆ cook: 1 hr., 40 min.
cool: 1 hr., 10 min.

1	lb. **butter,** softened		¾	cup **milk**
3	cups **sugar**		1	tsp. **almond extract**
6	large **eggs**		1	tsp. **vanilla extract**
4	cups **all-purpose flour**			

1. Preheat oven to 300°. Generously grease and lightly flour a 10-inch (14-cup) tube pan. Use shortening to grease the pan, covering bottom. Sprinkle a light coating of flour over the greased surface. Tap out any excess flour.

2. Beat butter at medium speed with an electric mixer until light yellow in color and creamy. Gradually add sugar, beating at medium speed until light and fluffy. Add eggs, 1 at a time, beating just until yellow disappears after each addition.

3. Add flour to butter mixture alternately with milk, beginning and ending with flour. Beat at low speed just until blended after each addition. (Batter should be smooth.) Stir in extracts. Pour batter into prepared pan.

4. Bake at 300° for 1 hour and 40 minutes or until a long wooden pick inserted in center comes out clean. Cool in pan on a wire rack 10 to 15 minutes. Remove from pan, and cool completely on wire rack (about 1 hour).

Note: Beating butter with a mixer will cause it to become a lighter yellow color; this is an important step, as the job of the mixer is to incorporate air into the butter so the cake will rise. It will take 1 to 7 minutes, depending on the power of your mixer.

German Chocolate Cheesecake

makes 12 servings ☆ prep: 30 min. ☆ cook: 52 min. ☆ chill: 8 hr.

1	cup **chocolate wafer crumbs**	⅓	cup **evaporated milk**
2	Tbsp. **sugar**	⅓	cup **sugar**
3	Tbsp. **butter,** melted	¼	cup **butter**
3	(8-oz.) packages **cream cheese,** softened	1	large **egg,** lightly beaten
¾	cup **sugar**	½	tsp. **vanilla extract**
¼	cup **unsweetened cocoa**	½	cup coarsely chopped **pecans,** toasted
2	tsp. **vanilla extract**	½	cup organic **coconut chips** or **sweetened flaked coconut**
3	large **eggs**		

With a nod to the classic three-layer cake, this luscious cheesecake takeoff comes pretty close to perfection.

1. Preheat oven to 325°. Stir together first 3 ingredients; press into bottom of an ungreased 9-inch springform pan.

2. Bake at 325° for 10 minutes. Cool crust.

3. Increase oven temperature to 350°. Beat cream cheese and next 3 ingredients at medium speed with an electric mixer until blended. Add eggs, 1 at a time, beating just until yellow disappears after each addition. Pour into prepared crust.

4. Bake at 350° for 35 minutes. Remove from oven; run a knife around edge of pan to loosen from sides of the pan. (Do not remove sides of pan.) Cool completely in pan on a wire rack. Cover and chill 8 hours.

5. Stir together evaporated milk and next 4 ingredients in a saucepan. Cook over medium heat, stirring constantly, 7 minutes. Stir in pecans and coconut. Remove sides of pan; spread topping over cheesecake.

Mixed-Berry Angel Cakes with Almond Sugar

makes 32 cupcakes ☆ prep: 25 min. ☆ chill: 1 hr. ☆ cook: 45 min.

1 (8-oz.) package **fresh strawberries** (about 1 cup), sliced

1 pt. **fresh blueberries** (about 1 cup)

1 (6-oz.) package **fresh raspberries** (about 1 cup)

⅔ cup **sugar**

¾ tsp. **almond extract**

1 (1-lb.) package **angel food cake mix**

Frozen whipped topping, thawed

1. Toss together berries. Stir together sugar and almond extract; sprinkle over berries, tossing to coat. Cover; chill 1 hour. Preheat oven to 350°. Prepare cake mix according to package directions.

2. Place paper baking cups in muffin pans; spoon batter into cups, filling two-thirds full. Bake, 1 muffin pan at a time, at 350° for 15 minutes or until lightly browned. Remove cupcakes from pans to wire racks; cool.

3. Cut cupcakes in half horizontally; spoon 1 Tbsp. berry mixture on bottom halves, and cover with tops. Spoon 1 Tbsp. berry mixture on top halves; dollop with whipped topping, and serve immediately.

Double Apple Pie with Cornmeal Crust

makes 8 servings ☆ prep: 30 min. ☆ stand: 30 min. ☆ cook: 1 hr., 20 min.
cool: 1 hr., 30 min. ☆ pictured on page 2

2¼	lb. Granny Smith apples		¼	tsp. ground nutmeg
2¼	lb. Braeburn apples		⅓	cup sugar
¼	cup all-purpose flour		**Cornmeal Crust Dough**	
2	Tbsp. apple jelly		3	Tbsp. sugar
1	Tbsp. fresh lemon juice		1	Tbsp. butter, cut into pieces
½	tsp. ground cinnamon		1	tsp. sugar
¼	tsp. salt		**Brandy-Caramel Sauce**	

1. Preheat oven to 425°. Peel and core apples; cut into ½-inch-thick wedges. Place in a large bowl. Stir in flour and next 6 ingredients. Let stand 30 minutes, gently stirring occasionally.

2. Place 1 Cornmeal Crust Dough disk on a lightly floured piece of wax paper; sprinkle dough lightly with flour. Top with another sheet of wax paper. Roll dough to about ⅛-inch thickness (about 11 inches wide).

3. Discard top sheet of wax paper. Starting at 1 edge of dough, wrap dough around rolling pin, separating dough from bottom sheet of wax paper as you roll. Discard wax paper. Place rolling pin over a 9-inch glass pie plate, and unroll dough over pie plate. Gently press dough into pie plate. Stir apple mixture; reserve 1 Tbsp. juices. Spoon apples into crust, packing tightly and mounding in center. Pour remaining juices in bowl over apples. Sprinkle apples with 3 Tbsp. sugar; dot with butter.

4. Roll remaining Cornmeal Crust Dough disk as directed in Step 2, rolling dough to about ⅛-inch thickness (11 inches wide). Remove and discard wax paper, and place dough over filling; fold edges under, sealing to bottom crust, and crimp. Brush top of pie, excluding fluted edges, lightly with reserved 1 Tbsp. juices from apples; sprinkle with 1 tsp. sugar. Place pie on a jelly-roll pan. Cut 4 or 5 slits in top of pie for steam to escape.

5. Bake at 425° on lower oven rack 15 minutes. Reduce oven temperature to 350°; transfer pie to middle oven rack, and bake 35 minutes. Cover loosely with aluminum foil to prevent excessive browning, and bake 30 more minutes or until juices are thick and bubbly, crust is golden brown, and apples are tender when pierced with a long wooden pick through slits in crust. Remove to a wire rack. Cool 1½ to 2 hours before serving. Serve with Brandy-Caramel Sauce.

Cornmeal Crust Dough

makes 2 dough disks ☆ prep: 15 min. ☆ chill: 1 hr.

2⅓ cups **all-purpose flour**

¼ cup **plain yellow cornmeal**

2 Tbsp. **sugar**

¾ tsp. **salt**

¾ cup cold **butter,** cut into
½-inch pieces

¼ cup chilled **shortening,** cut
into ½-inch pieces

8 to 10 Tbsp. chilled **apple
cider**

*For a flaky crust, make sure the
butter and shortening are cold.*

1. Stir together first 4 ingredients in a large bowl. Cut butter and shortening into flour mixture with a pastry blender until mixture resembles small peas. Mound mixture on 1 side of bowl.

2. Drizzle 1 Tbsp. apple cider along edge of mixture in bowl. Using a fork, gently toss a small amount of flour mixture into cider just until dry ingredients are moistened; move cider mixture to other side of bowl. Repeat procedure with remaining cider and flour mixture.

3. Gently gather dough into 2 flat disks. Wrap in plastic wrap, and chill 1 to 24 hours.

Brandy-Caramel Sauce

makes about 2 cups ☆ prep: 5 min. ☆ cook: 4 min. ☆ cool: 10 min.

1 cup **whipping cream**

1½ cups firmly packed **brown
sugar**

2 Tbsp. to ¼ cup **butter**

2 Tbsp. **brandy***

1 tsp. **vanilla extract**

1. Bring whipping cream to a light boil in a large saucepan over medium heat, stirring occasionally. Add sugar, and cook, stirring occasionally, 4 to 5 minutes or until sugar is dissolved and mixture is smooth. Remove from heat, and stir in butter, brandy, and vanilla. Let cool 10 minutes.

* Apple cider may be substituted.

Lemon Meringue Pie

makes 6 to 8 servings ☆ prep: 25 min. ☆ cook: 30 min.

Get ready for some down-home comfort with this tangy-tart lemon pie featuring a flaky crust. To cut clean slices, dip your knife blade into cold water between cuts.

½	(14.1-oz.) package **refrigerated piecrusts**	6	**egg whites**
	Lemon Meringue Pie Filling	½	tsp. **vanilla extract**
		6	Tbsp. **sugar**

1. Preheat oven to 450°. Fit piecrust into a 9-inch pie plate according to package directions; fold edges under, and crimp. Prick bottom and sides of piecrust with a fork.

2. Bake at 450° for 10 to 12 minutes or until lightly browned. Cool crust on a wire rack. Reduce oven temperature to 325°.

3. Prepare Lemon Meringue Pie Filling; remove from heat, and cover pan. (Proceed immediately to next step to ensure that meringue is spread over pie while filling is hot.)

4. Beat egg whites and vanilla at high speed with an electric mixer until foamy. Add sugar, 1 Tbsp. at a time, and beat until stiff peaks form. Pour hot filling into prepared crust. Spread meringue over filling, sealing edges.

5. Bake at 325° for 20 minutes or until golden. Cool pie completely on a wire rack. Store pie in refrigerator.

Lemon Meringue Pie Filling

makes enough for 1 (9-inch) pie ☆ prep: 10 min. ☆ cook: 10 min.

1	cup **sugar**	⅓	cup **fresh lemon juice**
¼	cup **cornstarch**	3	Tbsp. **butter**
⅛	tsp. **salt**	1	tsp. **lemon zest**
4	large **egg yolks**	½	tsp. **vanilla extract**
2	cups **milk**		

1. Whisk together first 3 ingredients in a medium-size heavy saucepan. Whisk in egg yolks, milk, and lemon juice. Bring to a boil over medium heat, whisking constantly. Cook, whisking constantly, 2 minutes; remove pan from heat. Stir in butter until melted; stir in lemon zest and vanilla.

Note: It's easier to remove the zest from lemons before juicing them.

Coconut Cream Pie

makes 8 servings ☆ prep: 20 min. ☆ cook: 13 min. ☆ cool: 5 min. ☆ chill: 4 hr.

½	(14.1-oz.) package **refrigerated piecrusts**
½	cup **sugar**
¼	cup **cornstarch**
2	cups **half-and-half**
4	**egg yolks**
3	Tbsp. **butter**
1	cup **sweetened flaked coconut**
2½	tsp. **vanilla extract**, divided
2	cups **whipping cream**
⅓	cup **sugar**
	Garnish: **toasted coconut**

In true diner style, this coconut pie has a thick, buttery filling and a mountain of whipped cream on top.

1. Preheat oven to 450°. Fit piecrust into a 9-inch pie plate according to package directions; fold edges under, and crimp. Prick bottom and sides of piecrust with a fork.

2. Bake at 450° for 10 to 12 minutes or until lightly browned. Cool crust on a wire rack.

3. Combine ½ cup sugar and cornstarch in a heavy saucepan. Whisk together half-and-half and egg yolks. Gradually whisk egg mixture into sugar mixture; bring to a simmer over medium heat, whisking constantly. Simmer, whisking constantly, 3 minutes; remove from heat. Stir in butter until it melts; stir in 1 cup coconut and 1 tsp. vanilla.

4. Place saucepan in an ice-water bath for 5 minutes or until filling is slightly warm, gently stirring occasionally. Pour filling into prepared crust. Place plastic wrap directly on custard (to prevent a film from forming). Place pie in refrigerator for 4 hours or until thoroughly chilled.

5. Beat whipping cream at high speed with an electric mixer until foamy; gradually add ⅓ cup sugar and remaining 1½ tsp. vanilla, beating until soft peaks form. Spread whipped cream over filling. Garnish, if desired.

Note: For dramatic effect, we garnished the pie with organic coconut chips. Find them at organic food stores. You could also use sweetened flaked coconut.

Classic Chess Pie

makes 1 (9-inch) pie ☆ prep: 23 min. ☆ cook: 56 min.

½	(14.1-oz.) package **refrigerated** **piecrusts**	½	cup **butter,** melted
2	cups **sugar**	¼	cup **milk**
2	Tbsp. **cornmeal**	1	Tbsp. **white vinegar**
1	Tbsp. **all-purpose flour**	½	tsp. **vanilla extract**
¼	tsp. **salt**	4	large **eggs,** lightly beaten

1. Preheat oven to 425°. Fit piecrust into a 9-inch pie plate according to package directions; fold edges under, and crimp. Line with aluminum foil; fill with pie weights or dried beans.

2. Bake at 425° for 4 to 5 minutes. Remove weights and foil; bake 2 more minutes or until golden. Cool. Reduce oven temperature to 350°.

3. Stir together sugar and next 7 ingredients until blended. Add eggs, stirring well. Pour into piecrust. Bake at 350° for 50 to 55 minutes, shielding edges with aluminum foil after 10 minutes to prevent excessive browning. Cool completely on a wire rack.

Bourbon-Chocolate-Pecan Tarts

makes 6 tarts ☆ prep: 15 min. ☆ chill: 30 min. ☆ cook: 30 min.

Try this wonderfully rich twist on a favorite Southern dessert.

Cream Cheese Pastry

¾ cup (4.5 oz.) **semisweet chocolate morsels**
3 large **eggs,** lightly beaten
⅓ cup **sugar**
3 Tbsp. firmly packed **light brown sugar**
1 Tbsp. **all-purpose flour**

¾ cup **light corn syrup**
¼ cup **butter,** melted
3 Tbsp. **bourbon**
2 tsp. **vanilla extract**
2 cups **pecan halves**
Garnishes: **whipped cream, pecan halves, chopped pecans** (optional)

1. Divide pastry into 6 portions, and shape each into a ball; press each into a 4½-inch tart pan. Sprinkle morsels over pastry; chill 30 minutes.

2. Preheat oven to 350°. Beat eggs and next 7 ingredients at medium speed with an electric mixer until blended. Pour into tart shells, filling each half full. Arrange pecan halves over filling; drizzle with remaining filling.

3. Bake at 350° for 30 to 35 minutes or until set; cool. Garnish, if desired.

Note: Tart filling may be baked in a 9-inch tart pan fitted with pastry crust. Prepare as directed; bake at 350° for 55 minutes or until set.

Cream Cheese Pastry

makes enough for 6 (4½-inch) tarts ☆ prep: 5 min.

1   (3-oz.) package **cream cheese,**   ½   cup **butter,** softened
    softened   1   cup **all-purpose flour**

1. Beat cream cheese and butter at medium speed with an electric mixer until smooth. Add flour; beat at low speed until a soft dough forms.

Easy Blackberry Cobbler

makes 6 servings ☆ prep: 10 min. ☆ cook: 35 min. ☆ stand: 10 min.

4	cups **fresh blackberries**		1	cup **all-purpose flour**
1	Tbsp. **lemon juice**		6	Tbsp. **butter**, melted
1	large **egg**			**Whipped cream** (optional)
1	cup **sugar**			Garnish: **fresh mint sprig**

Make the easiest blackberry cobbler ever using fresh berries plus 5 more ingredients. To make it special, top with whipped cream and a mint garnish.

1. Preheat oven to 375°. Place blackberries in a lightly greased 8-inch square baking dish; sprinkle with lemon juice. Stir together egg, sugar, and flour in a medium bowl until mixture resembles coarse meal. Sprinkle over fruit. Drizzle melted butter over topping. Bake at 375° for 35 minutes or until lightly browned and bubbly. Let stand 10 minutes. Serve warm with whipped cream, if desired. Garnish, if desired.

Note: For a neat presentation, bake for the same amount of time in 6 (8-oz.) ramekins on an aluminum foil–lined baking sheet.

Pecan-Peach Cobbler

makes 10 to 12 servings ☆ prep: 45 min. ☆ cook: 45 min.

This old-fashioned cobbler tempts your tastebuds with two Southern staples that always hit the spot—peaches and pecans.

12 to 15 **fresh peaches**, peeled and sliced (about 16 cups)
⅓ cup **all-purpose flour**
½ tsp. ground **nutmeg**
3 cups **sugar**
⅔ cup **butter**
1½ tsp. **vanilla extract**

2 (14.1-oz.) packages **refrigerated piecrusts**
½ cup chopped **pecans**, toasted and divided
5 Tbsp. **sugar**, divided
Garnish: **sweetened whipped cream**

1. Preheat oven to 475°. Stir together peaches, flour, nutmeg, and 3 cups sugar in a Dutch oven. Bring to a boil over medium heat; reduce heat to low, and simmer 10 minutes. Remove from heat; stir in butter and vanilla. Spoon half of mixture into a lightly greased 13- x 9-inch baking dish.

2. Unroll 2 piecrusts. Sprinkle ¼ cup pecans and 2 Tbsp. sugar over 1 piecrust; top with other piecrust. Roll into a 14- x 10-inch rectangle. Trim sides to fit baking dish. Place pastry over peach mixture in dish.

3. Bake at 475° for 20 to 25 minutes or until lightly browned. Unroll remaining 2 piecrusts. Sprinkle 2 Tbsp. sugar and remaining ¼ cup pecans over 1 piecrust; top with remaining piecrust. Roll into a 12-inch circle. Cut into 1-inch strips, using a fluted pastry wheel. Spoon remaining peach mixture over baked pastry. Arrange pastry strips over peach mixture; sprinkle with remaining 1 Tbsp. sugar. Bake 15 to 18 minutes or until lightly browned. Serve warm or cold with whipped cream, if desired.

Pound Cake Banana Pudding

makes 10 to 12 servings ☆ prep: 20 min. ☆ cook: 28 min. ☆ chill: 6 hr.

This recipe was inspired by the pudding served at the famous Mrs. Wilkes' Dining Room in Savannah, Georgia—a family-style, comfort-food restaurant to write home about.

4	cups **half-and-half**	3	Tbsp. **butter**
4	**egg yolks**	2	tsp. **vanilla extract**
1½	cups **sugar**	1	(1-lb.) **pound cake**, cubed
¼	cup **cornstarch**	4	large ripe **bananas**, sliced
¼	tsp. **salt**		**Meringue**

1. Whisk together first 5 ingredients in a saucepan over medium-low heat; cook, whisking constantly, 13 to 15 minutes or until thickened. Remove from heat; add butter and vanilla, stirring until butter melts.

2. Layer half of pound cake cubes, half of bananas, and half of pudding mixture in a lightly greased 3-qt. round baking dish. Repeat layers. Cover pudding, and chill 6 hours.

3. Preheat oven to 375°. Prepare Meringue, and spread over pudding.

4. Bake at 375° for 15 minutes or until golden brown. Spoon into glasses, if desired.

Note: We tested with Sara Lee Family Size All Butter Pound Cake.

Meringue

makes about 3½ cups ☆ prep: 10 min.

¼	cup **sugar**	4	**egg whites**
⅛	tsp. **salt**	¼	tsp. **vanilla extract**

1. Combine sugar and salt.

2. Beat egg whites and vanilla at high speed with an electric mixer until foamy. Add sugar mixture, 1 Tbsp. at a time, and beat 2 to 3 minutes or until stiff peaks form and sugar dissolves.

Creamy Rice Pudding with Praline Sauce

makes 6 to 8 servings ☆ prep: 15 min. ☆ cook: 50 min.

2	cups **milk**	4	**egg yolks**, beaten	
1	cup uncooked **extra long-grain white rice**	½	cup **sugar**	
½	tsp. **salt**	1½	tsp. **vanilla extract**	
2¾	cups **half-and-half**, divided	20	**caramels**	
		½	cup chopped toasted **pecans**	

If you're a fan of pure and simple old-fashioned desserts, this dish is for you. The praline sauce takes it to the next level.

1. Stir together first 3 ingredients and 2 cups half-and-half in a large saucepan. Cover and cook over medium-low heat, stirring often, 35 to 40 minutes or until rice is tender.

2. Whisk together egg yolks, ½ cup half-and-half, and sugar. Gradually stir about one-fourth of hot rice mixture into yolk mixture; stir yolk mixture into remaining hot mixture. Cook over medium-low heat, stirring constantly, until mixture reaches 160° and is thickened and bubbly (about 7 minutes). Remove from heat; stir in vanilla.

3. Stir together caramels and remaining ¼ cup half-and-half in a small saucepan over medium-low heat until smooth. Stir in pecans. Serve praline sauce over rice pudding.

Toffee-Oatmeal Cookies

makes 4 dozen ☆ prep: 14 min. ☆ cook: 10 min. per batch

½	cup **butter,** softened	1	cup **all-purpose flour**
½	cup firmly packed **brown sugar**	½	tsp. **baking soda**
2	large **eggs**	¼	tsp. **salt**
1	tsp. **vanilla extract**	½	cup chopped **pecans**
1½	cups uncooked **regular oats**	1½	cups (8 oz.) **toffee bits**

1. Preheat oven to 375°. Beat butter at medium speed with an electric mixer 2 to 3 minutes or until creamy. Add sugar, beating well. Add eggs and vanilla, beating until blended.

2. Combine oats and next 3 ingredients; add to butter mixture, beating just until blended. Stir in chopped pecans and toffee bits.

3. Drop dough by heaping tablespoonfuls onto lightly greased baking sheets.

4. Bake at 375° for 10 minutes. Remove to wire racks to cool completely.

10-Cup Cookies

makes 5½ dozen ☆ prep: 20 min. ☆ cook: 10 min. per batch

These cookies are chock-full of all the pantry's best flavors— nutty-tasting oats, pecans, coconut, raisins, and chocolate morsels. The recipe yields more than 5 dozen, so it's a great choice for taking to a cookie exchange party.

1 cup granulated sugar
1 cup firmly packed light brown sugar
1 cup shortening
1 cup peanut butter
3 large eggs, lightly beaten
1 cup all-purpose flour
1 cup uncooked quick-cooking oats

2 tsp. baking soda
1 tsp. baking powder
1 cup chopped pecans
1 cup sweetened flaked coconut
1 cup raisins
1 cup semisweet chocolate morsels

1. Preheat oven to 350°.

2. Combine first 4 ingredients in a large mixing bowl; beat at medium speed with an electric mixer until creamy. Add eggs, beating well.

3. Combine flour and next 3 ingredients; add to peanut butter mixture, and beat well. Stir in pecans and remaining ingredients. Drop dough by level teaspoonfuls onto lightly greased baking sheets.

4. Bake at 350° for 10 to 12 minutes or until golden. Immediately remove to wire racks to cool.

Soft Coconut Macaroons

makes about 3 dozen ☆ prep: 10 min. ☆ cook: 18 min. per batch

4   egg whites
2⅔   cups **sweetened flaked
        coconut**
⅔   cup **sugar**
¼   cup **all-purpose flour** or
        matzo meal

½   tsp. **clear vanilla extract**
¼   tsp. **salt**
¼   to ½ tsp. **almond extract**

1. Preheat oven to 325°. Stir together all ingredients in a large bowl, blending well. Drop dough by teaspoonfuls onto lightly greased baking sheets.

2. Bake at 325° for 18 to 20 minutes or until golden. Remove to wire racks to cool completely.

Note: Using clear vanilla extract will keep the macaroons pearly white, but if you don't have it, regular vanilla extract will work fine.

Blackberry-Lemon Squares

makes 2 dozen ☆ prep: 20 min. ☆ cook: 1 hr. ☆ cool: 1 hr.

2¼ cups all-purpose flour, divided
½ cup powdered sugar
1 cup cold butter, cut into pieces
4 large eggs
1½ cups granulated sugar
2 tsp. lemon zest
½ cup fresh lemon juice
1 tsp. baking powder
¼ tsp. salt
2 cups fresh blackberries
½ cup granulated sugar
Powdered sugar

1. Preheat oven to 350°. Line bottom and sides of a 13- x 9-inch pan with heavy-duty aluminum foil, allowing 2 to 3 inches to extend over sides; lightly grease foil.

2. Pulse 2 cups flour, ½ cup powdered sugar, and 1 cup butter in a food processor 5 or 6 times or until mixture is crumbly. Press mixture onto bottom of prepared pan.

3. Bake at 350° on lowest oven rack 25 minutes or just until golden brown.

4. Whisk together eggs and next 3 ingredients in a large bowl until blended. Combine baking powder, salt, and remaining ¼ cup flour; whisk into egg mixture until blended. Pour lemon mixture into prepared crust.

5. Pulse blackberries and ½ cup granulated sugar in a food processor 3 or 4 times or until blended. Transfer mixture to a small saucepan. Cook over medium-low heat, stirring often, 5 to 6 minutes or until thoroughly heated. Pour through a fine wire-mesh strainer into a bowl, gently pressing blackberry mixture with back of a spoon; discard solids. Drizzle over lemon mixture in pan.

6. Bake at 350° on middle oven rack 30 to 35 minutes or until filling is set. Let cool in pan on a wire rack 30 minutes. Lift from pan onto wire rack, using foil sides as handles, and let cool 30 minutes or until completely cool. Remove foil, and cut into 24 (2-inch) squares; sprinkle with powdered sugar.

So Good Brownies

makes 16 servings ☆ prep: 10 min. ☆ cook: 40 min. ☆ cool: 1 hr.

4	(1-oz.) unsweetened chocolate baking squares	3	large eggs
¾	cup butter	1	cup all-purpose flour
1½	cups granulated sugar	1	tsp. vanilla extract
½	cup firmly packed brown sugar	⅛	tsp. salt

1. Preheat oven to 350°. Line bottom and sides of an 8-inch pan with aluminum foil, allowing 2 to 3 inches to extend over sides; lightly grease foil.

2. Microwave chocolate squares and butter in a large microwave-safe bowl at HIGH 1½ to 2 minutes or until melted and smooth, stirring at 30-second intervals. Whisk in granulated and brown sugars. Add eggs, 1 at a time, whisking just until blended after each addition. Whisk in flour, vanilla, and salt.

3. Pour mixture into prepared pan.

4. Bake at 350° for 40 to 44 minutes or until a wooden pick inserted in center comes out with a few moist crumbs. Cool completely on a wire rack (about 1 hour). Lift brownies from pan, using foil sides as handles. Gently remove foil, and cut brownies into 16 squares.

Our Test Kitchen raves over this fudgy brownie recipe. This is our adaptation of a recipe many of our foodies use from Baker's Chocolate. Bonus? There are endless possible variations, including Caramel-Macchiato Brownies. Experiment with different additional ingredients to create something new and delicious with each pan.

variation

Caramel-Macchiato Brownies: Coffee fiends: Go with 1 Tbsp. espresso powder. Be advised—these are sticky! Avoid them if you wear braces. Prepare the brownie batter as directed through Step 2. Stir 1 cup miniature marshmallows, ½ cup caramel bits*, and 1½ tsp. to 1 Tbsp. instant espresso into batter. Increase bake time to 44 to 46 minutes.

*12 caramels, quartered, may be substituted.

Note: Be sure to insert wooden pick into brownie, not marshmallow, when testing for doneness. (Marshmallows will rise to the top when baking.) We tested with Kraft Caramel Bits.

Peanut Butter Squares

makes 2 dozen ☆ prep: 15 min. ☆ stand: 2 hr.

4   cups sifted **powdered sugar**
1   (5⅓-oz.) package **graham
     crackers,** crushed (about
     1⅔ cups)

1   cup **creamy peanut butter**
1   cup **butter,** melted
1   cup **semisweet chocolate
     morsels,** melted

By the late 1800s in the South, locally made peanut butter was sold door to door. It wasn't until the 1920s that peanut butter was produced commercially.

1. Stir together first 4 ingredients in a medium bowl. Firmly press mixture into an ungreased 13- x 9-inch pan. Spread melted chocolate evenly over cracker layer.

2. Let stand at room temperature 2 hours or until chocolate is set. Cut into squares.

make ahead

Layer Peanut Butter Squares between sheets of wax or parchment paper, and store in an airtight container up to 1 week, or freeze up to 1 month.

Oatmeal Carmelitas

makes 2 dozen ☆ prep: 25 min. ☆ cook: 34 min. ☆ stand: 1 min.

Cubes of chewy caramels provide the distinctive flavor for bar cookies also packed with chocolate morsels and pecans.

2	cups **all-purpose flour**
2	cups uncooked **quick-cooking oats**
1½	cups firmly packed **light brown sugar**
1	tsp. **baking soda**
¼	tsp. **salt**
1	cup **butter**, melted
1	(12-oz.) package **semisweet chocolate morsels**
½	cup chopped toasted **pecans** or **walnuts**, (optional)
1	(14-oz.) package **caramels**
⅓	cup **half-and-half**

1. Preheat oven to 350°.

2. Stir together first 5 ingredients in a large bowl. Add butter, stirring until mixture is crumbly. Set aside half of mixture (about 2¾ cups). Press remaining half of mixture into bottom of a lightly greased 13- x 9-inch pan. Sprinkle evenly with chocolate morsels, and, if desired, pecans.

3. Microwave caramels and half-and-half in a microwave-safe bowl at MEDIUM (50% power) 3 minutes. Stir and microwave at MEDIUM 1 to 3 more minutes or until mixture is smooth. Let stand 1 minute. Pour evenly over chocolate morsels. Sprinkle with reserved crumb mixture.

4. Bake at 350° for 30 minutes or until light golden brown. Cool completely in pan on a wire rack. Cut into bars.

make ahead

Have Oatmeal Carmelitas on hand for unexpected guests. Layer the bar cookies between sheets of parchment or wax paper, and seal in an airtight container. Store at room temperature up to a week, or freeze up to 1 month.

Salty Chocolate-Pecan Candy

makes 1¾ lb. ☆ prep: 10 min. ☆ cook: 13 min. ☆ chill: 1 hr.

This candy will soften slightly at room temperature.

1 cup **pecans,** coarsely chopped
3 (4-oz.) bars **bittersweet chocolate baking bars**
3 (4-oz.) **white chocolate baking bars**
1 tsp. **coarse sea salt***

1. Preheat oven to 350°. Place pecans in a single layer on a baking sheet.

2. Bake at 350° for 8 to 10 minutes or until toasted. Remove pecans from oven; set aside to cool. Reduce oven temperature to 225°.

3. Line a 17- x 12-inch jelly-roll pan with parchment paper. Break each chocolate bar into 8 equal pieces. (You will have 48 pieces total.) Arrange in a checkerboard pattern in jelly-roll pan, alternating white and dark chocolate. (Pieces will touch.)

4. Bake at 225° for 5 minutes or just until chocolate is melted. Remove pan to a wire rack. Swirl chocolates into a marble pattern using a wooden pick. Sprinkle evenly with toasted pecans and salt.

5. Chill 1 hour or until firm. Break into pieces. Store in an airtight container in refrigerator up to 1 month.

* ¾ tsp. kosher salt may be substituted.

Note: We tested with Ghirardelli 60% Cacao Bittersweet Chocolate Baking Bars and Ghirardelli White Chocolate Baking Bars.

Buckeye Balls

makes 7 dozen ☆ prep: 1 hr. ☆ chill: 10 min.

1 (16-oz.) jar **creamy peanut butter**

1 cup **butter,** softened

1½ (16-oz.) packages **powdered sugar**

2 cups (12 oz.) **semisweet chocolate morsels**

2 Tbsp. **shortening**

With only 5 ingredients, these candies are simple to make and taste divine.

1. Beat peanut butter and butter at medium speed with an electric mixer until blended. Gradually add powdered sugar, beating until blended.

2. Shape into 1-inch balls; chill 10 minutes or until firm.

3. Microwave chocolate and shortening in a microwave-safe 2-qt. glass bowl at HIGH 1½ minutes or until melted, stirring twice.

4. Dip each ball in chocolate mixture until partially coated; place on wax paper to harden. Store in an airtight container.

Metric Equivalents

The recipes that appear in this cookbook use the standard United States method for measuring liquid and dry or solid ingredients (teaspoons, tablespoons, and cups). The information on this chart is provided to help cooks outside the U.S. successfully use these recipes. All equivalents are approximate.

Metric Equivalents for Different Types of Ingredients

A standard cup measure of a dry or solid ingredient will vary in weight depending on the type of ingredient. A standard cup of liquid is the same volume for any type of liquid. Use the following chart when converting standard cup measures to grams (weight) or milliliters (volume).

Standard Cup	Fine Powder (ex. flour)	Grain (ex. rice)	Granular (ex. sugar)	Liquid Solids (ex. butter)	Liquid (ex. milk)
1	140 g	150 g	190 g	200 g	240 ml
¾	105 g	113 g	143 g	150 g	180 ml
⅔	93 g	100 g	125 g	133 g	160 ml
½	70 g	75 g	95 g	100 g	120 ml
⅓	47 g	50 g	63 g	67 g	80 ml
¼	35 g	38 g	48 g	50 g	60 ml
⅛	18 g	19 g	24 g	25 g	30 ml

Useful Equivalents for Liquid Ingredients by Volume

¼ tsp						=	1 ml	
½ tsp						=	2 ml	
1 tsp						=	5 ml	
3 tsp	=	1 Tbsp			=	½ fl oz	=	15 ml
		2 Tbsp	=	⅛ cup	=	1 fl oz	=	30 ml
		4 Tbsp	=	¼ cup	=	2 fl oz	=	60 ml
		5⅓ Tbsp	=	⅓ cup	=	3 fl oz	=	80 ml
		8 Tbsp	=	½ cup	=	4 fl oz	=	120 ml
		10⅔ Tbsp	=	⅔ cup	=	5 fl oz	=	160 ml
		12 Tbsp	=	¾ cup	=	6 fl oz	=	180 ml
		16 Tbsp	=	1 cup	=	8 fl oz	=	240 ml
		1 pt	=	2 cups	=	16 fl oz	=	480 ml
		1 qt	=	4 cups	=	32 fl oz	=	960 ml
						33 fl oz	=	1000 ml = 1 l

Useful Equivalents for Dry Ingredients by Weight

(To convert ounces to grams, multiply the number of ounces by 30.)

1 oz	=	¹⁄₁₆ lb	=	30 g
4 oz	=	¼ lb	=	120 g
8 oz	=	½ lb	=	240 g
12 oz	=	¾ lb	=	360 g
16 oz	=	1 lb	=	480 g

Useful Equivalents for Length

(To convert inches to centimeters, multiply the number of inches by 2.5.)

1 in				=	2.5 cm		
6 in	=	½ ft		=	15 cm		
12 in	=	1 ft		=	30 cm		
36 in	=	3 ft	= 1 yd	=	90 cm		
40 in				=	100 cm	=	1 m

Useful Equivalents for Cooking/Oven Temperatures

	Fahrenheit	Celsius	Gas Mark
Freeze water	32° F	0° C	
Room temperature	68° F	20° C	
Boil water	212° F	100° C	
Bake	325° F	160° C	3
	350° F	180° C	4
	375° F	190° C	5
	400° F	200° C	6
	425° F	220° C	7
	450° F	230° C	8
Broil			Grill

Index